THE LAST PRAIRIE

A Sandhills Journal

S T E P H E N R. J O N E S

University of Nebraska Press   Lincoln

First Nebraska paperback printing: 2006

Acknowledgments for previously published material begin on page 230.
Design and illustratons by Dennis Anderson
Nebraska map by Shane Reiswig

Library of Congress Cataloging-in-Publication Data
Jones, Stephen R., 1947–
The last prairie: a Sandhills journal / Stephen R. Jones.
p. cm.
Originally published: Camden, Me.: Ragged Mountain Press, c2000.
ISBN-13: 978-0-8032-7630-7 (pbk.: alk. paper)
ISBN-10: 0-8032-7630-3 (pbk.: alk. paper)
1. Natural history—Nebraska—Sandhills. 2. Prairie ecology—Nebraska—
Sandhills. 3. Sandhills (Neb.)—History. I. Title.
QH105.N2J66 2006
508.782—dc22 2005023827

For my parents, Kay and Bill

CONTENTS

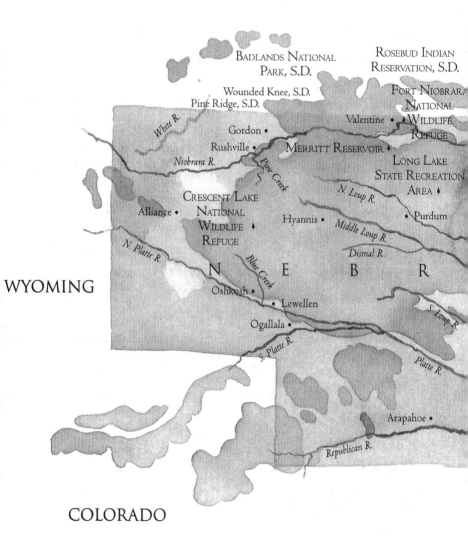

SOUTH DAKOTA

BADLANDS NATIONAL
PARK, S.D.

ROSEBUD INDIAN
RESERVATION, S.D.

Wounded Knee, S.D.
Pine Ridge, S.D.

FORT NIOBRARA
NATIONAL
WILDLIFE
REFUGE

Valentine •

White R.

Gordon •

MERRITT RESERVOIR ◆

Rushville •

Niobrara R.

LONG LAKE
STATE RECREATION
AREA ◆

Pine Creek

N. Loup R.

CRESCENT LAKE
NATIONAL
WILDLIFE ◆
REFUGE

Alliance •

Hyannis •

Purdum

Middle Loup R.

Dismal R.

N. Platte R.

N   E   B   R.

Blue Creek

Oshkosh •

• Lewellen

Ogallala •

S. Loup R.

WYOMING

S. Platte R.

Platte R.

Arapahoe •

Republican R.

COLORADO

Shaded areas represent the extent of the
Nebraska Sandhills and neighboring sand hills

INTRODUCTION

AN ARAPAHO story tells of a peaceful land just beyond a distant hill. When we feel death approaching, we make our way up the hill. From the crest we gaze down on a shimmering valley where the grass grows thick and green. A broad river flows there. Children and wild horses frolic in the sparkling current. The way down is easy, but the people on the living side of the hill hold onto us with all their will, begging us to turn back. The decision to continue or return is the toughest and most painful challenge we ever face, but we must go on. As we walk down into the valley, people from all the generations gather to welcome us. Mother Earth holds us in her heart and soothes our sorrow.

For years, I've been haunted by that story. I've longed for the sense of peace in nature and acceptance of fate that the legend evokes, and I've searched for a living version of that peaceful valley beyond that distant hill.

I grew up among sprawling suburbs south of San Francisco, a few miles from the majestic oak savannas and redwood forests of the Pacific Coast Range. I daydreamed my way through school, frequently imagining I was somewhere "out there," fishing with my father or flushing mule deer and bobcats from the chaparral.

After completing college in 1970, I migrated to Boulder, Colorado, a quiet university town encircled by mountains, grasslands, and farms. I made my way in Boulder as a school-teacher and naturalist, taking advantage of the miles of hiking trails and open space that surround our community.

But the more I learned about nature, the more painful it became to live in Boulder as our local population exploded and the burgeoning Denver suburbs closed in. I saw golden eagles chased off their nests by rock climbers and watched terrified mule deer flee from packs of domestic dogs. I felt my stomach tighten as prairie dog colonies and farm-land vanished under a relentless tide of subdivisions and shopping malls. Even our mountains—crowded with off-road vehicles, scarred by ski areas and condominiums—felt claustrophobic.

Then I discovered the prairie, and a slow healing began. I fell in love with the fiery sunrises, supple grasses waving in the wind, the abundant wildlife and boundless space. I spent idyllic mornings searching for arrowheads in the grass, exploring old homesteads, conversing with farmers and ranchers whose families had worked the same land for more than a century.

One morning I found some fossilized clam shells lying in the buffalo grass and the entire skeleton of a pronghorn antelope embedded in the chalky bank of a dry ravine. Later, I walked through an isolated grove of limber pines, a last relict of the coniferous forests that covered the plains 15,000 years ago. I began to understand that the grass around me, the limber pines, the clams and 80-million-year-old ocean that spawned them, and I were all made from the same stuff, our lives woven together by the same currents of time and place. I felt comforted and liberated.

I traveled from Texas to North Dakota searching for an expanse of prairie, a natural grassland stretching from horizon to horizon. One ethereal May evening I chanced upon Crescent Lake National Wildlife Refuge, in the western Sandhills. I watched the sun settle down into a sea of grassy hills and knew I'd found the place.

I continue to live and work in Boulder, but I spend several weeks each year in the Sandhills camping alone, walking under the stars, immersing myself in local history and Plains Indian creation stories. My love for the Sandhills has grown to a passion, and so have my fears that the forces that drove me to this place of sanctuary will eventually destroy it.

Recently, I stood on a wind-sculpted ridge with a friend, a Native American holy man, admiring the surrounding countryside and reflecting on its hypnotic appeal. "The Sandhills," he said, "is the most sacred of all places. It's where our spirit goes to rest when we die."

As we stood there with the wind whipping through our hair and nothing visible but grass, water, and sky, I knew his words were true.

LANDMARKS

*We could feel the peace and power of the Great Mystery
in the soft grass under our feet and in the blue sky
above us. All this made deep feeling within us, and this
is how we got our religion.*

—Luther Standing Bear, *My Indian Boyhood*

THE MAIN highway north from Oshkosh, Nebraska, feels eerily deserted as I drive up out of the Platte River Valley and ease my way into the Sandhills. I meet no vehicles along the narrow roadway. No humans stir in the meadows and hills.

The road winds past abandoned farmhouses with tumbleweeds stacked three deep on their front porches, over sparsely vegetated knolls where curlews and horned larks scatter in the wind, and down into luxuriant valleys flecked with shallow lakes and ponds. A herd of mule deer watches from a ridge top. Kangaroo rats and cottontails scamper across the cracked asphalt. As the high cirrus clouds drift slowly eastward and Swainson's hawks circle overhead, the sky stretches out and the hills roll away toward infinity.

For miles the road runs unfettered over the grasslands, with no fences on either side and not a highway sign or settlement in sight. I cruise past meadows of ripening hay and thread my way through herds of sleepy cattle, stopping briefly to brush up on my Hereford and to photograph an eastern kingbird perched on a yucca stalk. As always when driving this empty stretch, I'm tempted to take a hard right and disappear completely into the sea of sweet green grass, cool hollows, and sun-washed dunes.

There are plenty of Sandhills to get lost in. Encompassing about one-fourth of the state of Nebraska, they are the largest area of grass-stabilized dunes in the Western Hemisphere. The Sandhills stretch two hundred miles from west to east and one hundred miles from south to north, from the Platte River in central Nebraska to the Niobrara River near the South Dakota border.

The dunes are covered almost entirely with native grasses: big bluestem, sand bluestem, little bluestem, prairie sandreed, switchgrass. This Sandhills prairie, with its unique mosaic of grasses, wildflowers, shallow lakes, and spring-fed streams, is the largest remaining relict of the boundless grasslands that once extended from the Missouri River to the Rocky Mountains.

The Sandhills support more pelicans than people. The human population, which rose briefly during the early years of white settlement, has declined steadily since the 1920s and currently stands at about one inhabitant per square mile. Tourists are scarcer than the few pronghorn antelope that wander among the hills.

Sandhills residents, mostly ranchers, interact quietly with nature every day. A typical Sandhills ranch covers from 2,000 to 100,000 acres. Some ranchers use airplanes and helicopters to keep track of their herds. Sandhills residents may drive thirty miles or more to "town"—sometimes a gas station and general store, a post office, and a handful of weather-beaten frame houses. Blizzards can leave ranches isolated for days or weeks.

City dwellers who visit the region quickly become unnerved by the near absence of trees, the vast distance between settlements, and the sameness of the rolling landscape. Some find the quiet disquieting. During my first few visits I experienced a persistent ringing in the ears as my hearing adjusted to the absence of background noise—the roar of cars, airplanes, and machinery that has become a subliminal part of our daily lives.

This morning, as I admire the June-green grasses along the road, the ringing in my ears has subsided, and I notice sounds that barely registered before, like the "click ... click" of grasshoppers in the little bluestem and the whir of ducks' wings on a distant lake. At dawn this morning, when swallowtails clung to glistening grasses and the valley fog turned gold in the sunlight, I could just make out the grunts and bellows of bison lumbering along the ridge tops and the laughing of Cheyenne, Lakota, and Pawnee children playing in sunflower meadows.

By the time the Oshkosh–Lakeside road reaches Crescent Lake National Wildlife Refuge, twenty-eight miles north of Oshkosh, it has degenerated into a one-lane "oil road," a thin layer of soft asphalt mixed from sand and oil and plastered onto the landscape. Steeply crowned, with chunks of asphalt sloughing off on either side like pieces of a jigsaw puzzle, the pothole-strewn highway rattles across alkali flats and bounces over narrow cattle guards framed by giant truck tires. With no conventional landmarks visible and a confusion of hills rolling and tumbling in every direction, time and distance are marked by the lakes, several hundred of them within a few miles of the roadway.

Schoonover Lake, Floyd Lake, Old Woman Lake, Peter Long Lake; Sand Beach, Swan, and Alkali Lakes; Black Steer Lake, Wild Horse Lake, and Bean Can Lake. Long-time Sandhills residents can recite the history of the region through the names of its lakes and valleys. In Custer County folks tell how Richard Greenland, one of the founders of Purdum, came across a Pawnee skull while out hunting. The location of this rather modest 110-year-old discovery is emblazoned on the map as Skull Lake. Residents of Sheridan County know that Elk Valley was christened in 1888 when two hunters from Omaha slaughtered the last elk ever seen in the region, and that Alkali Lake was where Joseph Adkins had to dig five feet down in 1880 to find water for coffee.

Today I set out to explore as many of these romantically named spots as I can locate. The attractions generally consist of a wild, empty landscape with a weathered signboard or two pointing to the nearest ranch. But it's reassuring to discover places that have hardly changed since the day they were named.

At Island Lake I find eared grebes hunkered down on floating nests; at Black Lake, a baby pronghorn and a pair of trumpeter swans; at Goose Lake, a two-foot-long snapping turtle waddling through a patch of honey-scented sand verbena. I encounter no humans and few human footprints.

I stop for lunch at Wood Lake, a briny pond surrounded by mudflats and sedge-rush meadows—and the site of an avocet convention. Several dozen of the blue-legged, rufous-necked shorebirds wade in the shallows, swishing their upturned beaks back and forth to seine invertebrates from the water.

I flatten out in the moist grass and slither down toward shore to photograph a couple of young avocets. Within seconds a score of adults have me surrounded. They strut back and forth, bleating obstreperously, and skitter across the salt flats, feigning injury. Two particularly audacious birds come charging forward, screaming bloody murder and snapping their wings menacingly.

I apologize and shuffle back to the car. A box turtle has parked in the shade under the front bumper. I pick him up, set him gently on the shoulder, and watch as he gingerly pokes his wizened, greenish yellow head out from his ornate carapace. He blinks a grain of sand from a moist eye, slowly extends his neck, and plods off into the long grass.

A sandy two-track road winds toward Crane Lake, a blue oasis among soft green hills. The "cranes" turn out to be a colony of great blue herons. The adults perch atop a dozen bulky stick nests in a small grove of half-dead cottonwoods. The herons fuss and squawk as I approach along a cattle trail framed by swaying stalks of switchgrass and sand bluestem.

An adult flies in with a carp flopping in its bill. Two gaping, orange-tinged beaks appear above the edge of one nest, and the squawking rises in a crescendo. The parent stuffs pieces of carp into the youngsters' throats, pushes off, and flaps away toward the lakeshore.

At dusk I sit on a hillside as crickets begin their rhythmic chirruping and nighthawks swoop overhead. A pair of coyotes amble down the cattle trail, stopping every few yards to lap up a grasshopper or two. A pelican squadron glides over the rookery, skims across the water, and splashes down against the far shore. Curlews wail their approval.

As I walk away from the lake, I feel the wild sounds and calming space of the prairie drawing me back. This would be a fine night to hide out in the long grass, bed down with the mule deer, maybe den up with a coyote or two.

My first howl elicits a response. They're somewhere off beyond the water, lost in the dwindling light. The whole family yips in concert, calling up the moon, stars, and kindred spirits while I listen and wait.

ANCIENT VOICES

ON A CRISP, late October morning, I pack my rucksack and head down the sand trail to Lower Harrison Lake, near the western edge of Crescent Lake National Wildlife Refuge. It's one of those sumptuous fall days—its dazzle heightened by the proximity of winter—with not a hint of wind, not a speck of cloud in the cobalt sky. The hills bask in amber light, and deep shadows linger in the hollows.

Swarms of red-winged blackbirds swirl over the marshes, mixing with swift-flying flocks of Canada geese, redheads, and shovelers. A pheasant bolts from the tall grass, crowing and cackling frantically. Two marsh hawks cruise by, tilting their wings from side to side, listening, while scurrying meadow voles send shivers through the ripening grasses and brittle cattails.

My destination is a group of nearly conical hills pockmarked with blowouts, craterlike depressions carved out by the wind. Blowouts support one of Nebraska's rarest and most striking plants, the lavender-colored, vanilla-scented Hayden's blowout penstemon. Badgers and coyotes den in the steep banks, and deer mice and beetles create a frieze of artfully etched tracks. These sand craters also provide great sunbathing, with fine, clean sand like a tropical beach. A secluded blowout seems the perfect place to spend the last warm day of the season.

The hills lie on the far side of a wet meadow where the switchgrass and big bluestem grow head high. I swish through the grass, unable to see the ground, reassuring myself that rattlesnakes avoid moist areas. A huge animal explodes from the grass, almost knocking me over. I catch my balance as a four-point whitetail buck rockets across the meadow, stops at the edge, then bounds up into the hills. The last sight of him is his snow-white tail, held high in alarm, bobbing up and down against the azure horizon.

Once into the hills, I find a steep-walled crater about fifty feet across, take off most of my clothes, and settle into the cool sand. Lying in the blowout is like being in an observatory, with a circle of sky overhead. Way up there, a pair of ferruginous hawks float back and forth, their underwings and breasts sparkling white in the sunlight, as I drift off to sleep.

A faint, rhythmic trilling ripples the still air. I open my eyes and scan the sky. Nothing but blue. But the trilling grows louder, becoming an insistent, pulsating rattle. I begin to recognize the sound, just as almost anyone would know the buzz of a rattlesnake or the hoot of an owl. But I can't put a name to it right away. It registers only as something old, familiar, and wild.

Finally a hundred or more silvery specks come into view straight overhead. Sandhill cranes. They're visible for just an instant before being swallowed up in the blue. A few seconds later the cranes materialize again as they wheel around and the sun reflects off their steel-blue feathers. The show repeats itself over and over, the cranes vanishing and reappearing, circling higher and higher on the thermals rising over the dunes. After a few minutes their vocalizations become more urgent, and they sail off south.

For the next several hours the cranes come in wave after wave. I count hundreds, then tens of thousands. Some pass so close I can see their crimson crests. Others fly so high I can only hear them.

This migration flight originated north of the Arctic Circle, in northern Canada, Alaska, and eastern Siberia, where most of these cranes spent the summer raising their young. The flocks are bound for Texas and the Gulf Coast, where family groups will pass the winter feeding on crabs, snails, and other invertebrates in estuaries and foraging for grain in the adjacent fields. Tonight they'll sleep on the Platte, roosting on islands or in shallows safe from predators. Within a few days they'll continue south toward the Arkansas and Republican Rivers.

Sandhill cranes have been making this migration for eons. The fossil record in Nebraska goes back about 9 million years. They are among the most ancient of North American birds. Their voices trumpeted across this part of North America long before the Sandhills came into being.

Three million years ago, cranes migrating over what is now western Nebraska looked down on a landscape of humid forests, swamps, and open meadows populated by stegomastodons, camels, zebralike horses, giant beavers, and tortoises. Sabertooth cats stalked the forest clearings, and enormous ground sloths ambled through dense, mossy thickets.

Thirty thousand years ago, migrating cranes rested on sandbars in the middle of several shallow, braided rivers that flowed over sandy plains. Bison, pronghorn, elk, and bighorn sheep mixed in with the camels, horses, and mammoths that grazed in savannas and pine forests bordering the water. Giant prairie lions hunted among these mixed herds, while chill breezes blew off of glaciers that extended southward within a few hundred miles of present-day western Nebraska. The modern Platte and Niobrara River Valleys had not yet formed, nor had the Sandhills.

About 10,000 to 15,000 years ago, toward the end of the last ice age, migrating cranes encountered Clovis hunters, nomadic people who followed the mammoths, mastodons, and sloths, possibly hunting them to extinction. It was then, as the climate warmed, that fierce northwesterly winds began to mold alluvial deposits into the dunes that now cover much of western Nebraska.

About 150 years ago, the cranes encountered the first white settlers on the Great Plains. After surviving millions of years of geologic and climatic change, these resilient birds nearly vanished within a few decades. Hunters killed hundreds of thousands. Later, dam and irrigation projects threatened to drain away rivers essential to the cranes' survival.

The most critical of these dwindling waterways is the Platte. Each spring half a million cranes, 80 percent of the world's population, gather along a two-hundred-mile stretch of the river to rest and refuel during their northward migration. Wetlands adjacent to the river teem with amphibians and invertebrates, a bounty of protein and calories sufficient to sustain the birds through the stressful summer nesting period when they have little time to forage. But water projects have diminished the flow of the once broad Platte to one or two narrow channels. Without the scouring of spring floods, the cranes' sandbar roosts are becoming choked with vegetation. Conservationists working in a handful of small wildlife refuges struggle to preserve the remaining roosts.

One frigid evening in late March I stood on the banks of the Platte with Ken Strom, director of the Lillian Annette Rowe Audubon Sanctuary near Kearney. Ken is a broad-shouldered, serious, and soft-spoken man who has fought for twenty years to preserve crane habitat along the river. On spring field trips he takes people from all over the world down to the riverside blinds to watch the flocks gather at sunset and disperse at sunrise. Ken answers each question slowly and thoughtfully, as if hearing it for the first time. He speaks of the cranes with awe and respect.

"I never get tired of the cranes, and I get excited each spring when they come back. I think, more than anything, it's their call. It's very wild and also very ancient. Cranes flew over the dinosaurs. Their voices are our closest link to prehistoric times."

Ken talked about educating the local farmers, many of whom gave little thought to the cranes until the tourists began showing up a decade or two ago.

"I've seen farmers who would have been perfectly happy to do away with cranes in the name of progress, but when they come down to the river and see the great flocks, they come away saying, 'What can we do to help? We have no right to destroy this.'"

He led us out to a bluff overlooking the river and pointed to a hill half a mile away.

"That was the far shore, and the river in between was a series of braided channels interspersed with sandbars. Now, as you can see, the remaining channel here is only about a hundred yards across. We have to burn or cut brush from the remaining sandbars each year to keep the roosts open."

With the sun balanced on the western horizon and the sky gray with cranes, we walked to a two-story plywood blind overlooking the south channel. We watched in silence as clouds of the majestic birds rose from the cornfields and tallgrass meadows beside the river, circled, arched their wings, and parachuted down to their roosts. Ken suggested we cup our hands behind our ears to amplify their voices. It was spine chilling, nearly deafening—the primeval sound of spring returning to the sandbars and channels of the Platte River.

Native Americans didn't need endangered species lists or environmental impact studies to tell them cranes were valuable and sacred. Some Cheyenne warriors decorated their shields with the feathers, skins, and heads of sandhill cranes. They made war whistles from the cranes' wing bones, and warriors who imitated the cry of the crane as they rode into battle were thought to be bulletproof.

According to Pueblo Indian legend, cranes once lived in the clouds, where they nested and drank the water that falls from the heavens. But they grew tired of the easy life and descended to earth where there were fishes and frogs to eat. The enormous flock of cranes moved from desert spring to desert spring, exhausting the food and water as they traveled, until they came to the great valley of the Rio Grande. There they made their permanent camp, from which they spread out over the earth.

A Cree story tells how rabbit yearned to fly to the moon. He asked all the great birds to take him there. All refused except Crane. Crane told Rabbit to hold onto his legs. But Rabbit was very heavy, and as he held on, Crane's legs stretched out farther and farther. When Crane and Rabbit reached the moon, Rabbit touched Crane's head and gave him a dazzling red headdress as a reward. They say that if you look when the moon is full, you can still see Rabbit riding on the moon. Crane's legs remain long and straight, and his head is forever red.

In Africa, in Asia, in Aboriginal Australia, people have worshiped cranes and adopted them as pets or good-luck charms. Aldo Leopold cut to the heart of this universal relationship between people and cranes in *A Sand County Almanac*: "Our appreciation of the crane grows with the slow unraveling of earthly history. His tribe, we now know, stems out of the remote Eocene. The other members of the fauna in which he originated are long since entombed within the hills. When we hear his call we hear no mere bird. He is the symbol of our untamable past, of that incredible sweep of millennia which underlies and conditions the daily affairs of birds and men."

AFTER DRIFTING in and out of sleep for several hours, soothed by the pulsating voices of the cranes, I'm jolted awake by a sharp yipping and the sound of something scrambling up the side of the dune. I jump into my clothes just as the face of a panting, flop-eared spaniel appears over the edge. She's soon joined by a man dressed in fatigues and carrying a shotgun.

"Have you seen any grouse?"

"Only one," I mumble, pointing vaguely in the general direction of Wyoming.

He thanks me and heads off that way. I climb up out of the blowout and look around. The cranes are gone.

As I descend through the dunes, the cool sand sifts into my boot tops and the feathery seed heads of the bluestem tickle the hairs on my bare arms. A whitetail doe and her fawn watch from a nearby ridge. The hills roll away like restless swells on a golden sea.

The next morning I drive up to the Niobrara River, east of Valentine. I park at the old Norden Bridge, where the river plunges through a narrow chute and rushes out onto a broad channel flanked by sandstone cliffs and musty forests of ponderosa pine, bur oak, paper birch, and linden.

At sunset I climb up a hill to watch the full moon rise over the valley. A flock of cranes comes sailing in from the north. They glide across the face of the moon, circle overhead, and float down to the river like dry autumn leaves.

I lay out my sleeping bag on the grassy riverbank and fall asleep to the murmurings of the Niobrara, the cries of screech-owls, and the rhythmic crane song. When I wake in the night my bedding glistens with frost. Orion's bright figure hovers over the shadowy bluffs on the opposite shore. The cranes rattle softly somewhere downriver.

FOUR WINDS

Everything the Power of the World does is done in a circle. The sky is round, and I have heard that the earth is round like a ball, and so are all the stars. The wind, in its greatest power, whirls. . . . The sun comes forth and goes down again in a circle. The moon does the same, and both are round. Even the seasons form a circle in their changing, and always come back to where they were.

—Black Elk, *Black Elk Speaks*

IN THE EARLY days Tate, the wind, and his five sons lived where the waving grasses of the prairie meet the cool shadows of the pine forest. Their lodge faced the midday sun, whose light shone through the entrance, illuminating the place of honor where Tate sat. Beside him sat Yata, his firstborn son; to his right, Eya, his second born; to his left, Yanpa, his third born; and before him, close to the door, Okaga, his fourth born. The youngest son, Yum, sat in the woman's place by the fire, close to his loving brother Okaga.

The sunlight felt warm and comforting. At night the

stars shone down, bringing wisdom and life. The moon circled overhead, waxing and waning as the days and nights passed.

Each dawn the three oldest brothers walked off from the lodge and dispersed over the world to find food. Okaga stayed home tending the fire, hauling wood and water, and caring for his innocent, perpetually childlike brother Yum.

One day when all the sons were away, a star fell from the sky and landed close to the lodge. When Tate walked over to look, he found an enchanting young woman wearing a soft white dress. He asked where she had come from.

"I came from the sky," she said, "My people are the stars."

"Why have you come to us?"

"My father, Skan, sent me to the world to bring a token to you."

Tate said, "I will be your godfather. Live with me in my lodge as long as you wish, but do not tell my sons where you came from or who you are."

The beautiful star child, Wohpe, entered the lodge, tak-.ing a seat at the woman's place by the fire. When the sons returned, she greeted them affectionately and used her magic powers to produce an endless supply of their favorite delicacies. She said she would always be a sister to them so long as they treated her as a sister.

The next day Wohpe sat down with her godfather and delivered Skan's message. She explained that there were now only three units of time: the day, the night, and the moon. Tate and his sons were to establish the fourth unit.

To do this the sons must place four directions equal distances apart on the edge of the earth. The first direction would lie where the sun casts its longest shadow; the second direction, where the sun rises each morning; the third direction, where the sun stands overhead at midday; the fourth direction, where the sun sets at night.

The young men were to travel around the edge of the earth, establishing the directions one by one. When they finished their journey, the fourth unit of time, the year, would be complete.

"You shall govern the fourth time and shall give a part of this time to each of your four sons," she said.

For twelve moons Tate's oldest sons traveled along the edge of the earth, encountering wizards and great beasts of every description and surviving many encounters with Iktomi, the spider trickster.

Yata, the most vain, covetous, and irritable, fixed his direction where the sun casts its longest shadow. He became the North Wind, and his messenger is the magpie, which is disagreeable and fouls its nest.

Yanpa fixed his direction where the sun rises each morning. He became the East Wind, and his messenger is the crow.

Okaga established his direction where the sun passes overhead at midday. He became the South Wind, and his messenger is the meadowlark, whose bright yellow breast mirrors the sun.

Eya established his direction on the mountainside where the sun sets each night. He became the West Wind, companion to the winged god. His messenger is the swift-flying swallow.

When the four sons returned to Tate's lodge, Wohpe greeted them with a tender smile. They became infatuated and began to fight over her.

The North Wind went hunting and brought game, but it quickly turned to ice.

The West Wind pounded his drum and sang to her, but he made such a racket that the tipi fell down.

The East Wind sat down and talked endless nonsense, nearly driving her to tears.

The South Wind played his flute and made her beautiful things. She chose him for her husband.

As Okaga led Wohpe away, the North Wind tried to steal her from him. The South Wind resisted, pushing the North Wind back with a strong, hot blast. While the North Wind and South Wind struggled and blustered over Wohpe, she spread her dress out over the earth and crawled underneath so they could not find her.

The North Wind blew icy gusts over her, freezing the billowing dress. The South Wind fought back, warming the dress and melting the ice. The East Wind and the West Wind joined in the struggle. Yum danced in circles, creating little whirlwinds.

Thus was born the battle of the Winds, which continues to this day.

IN LATER years the people who traced their creation to the marriage of the stars and winds worshiped the four directions with a reverence that was incomprehensible to many other peoples. To the Lakota the winds that swept over the prairie were far more than meteorological phenomena. The sun, moon, and stars were far more than celestial objects. All were flesh, blood, and spirit. In *Sacred Ways of a Lakota*, shaman Wallace Black Elk writes, "The powers of the Four Winds are your relatives. Pray to them. Talk to them. They are your relatives."

Another Lakota shaman, John Lame Deer, put it less formally: "Here, in South Dakota, they say, 'If you don't like the weather, wait five minutes.' It can be 100 degrees in the shade one afternoon and suddenly there comes a storm with hailstones as big as golf balls, the prairie is all white and your teeth chatter. That's good—a reminder that you are just a small particle of nature, not so powerful as you think."

In the Sandhills prairie the four directions assert themselves with a vengeance. With no obstacles to dampen their energy, the winds bear down from Canada, rush outward from the Rockies, and sweep north from the Gulf of Mexico. Cold fronts racing across the region every three to five days turn the seasons upside down as strong, hot southerlies give way to face-numbing northerlies. Warm "chinooks" blowing down from the Rockies can dissolve six inches of snow in minutes. In early spring fifty-mile-an-hour winds buffet the prairie for days on end.

For travelers in these hills the winds can be annoying at the very least. It's more than the inconvenience of waking up in April wrapped in a frozen tent or having your windshield shattered by softball-sized hailstones in July. The daily buffeting makes you disoriented and irritable. Many of the wild creatures react the same way. On blustery days, white-tailed deer and pronghorn grow skittish, Swainson's hawks hole up in shrub thickets, and normally complacent coyotes scurry away at the slightest provocation. Birds and mammals have learned to distrust this force that confounds the senses of hearing and smell so vital for their survival in the wild. So have I. When the winds howl at night, my childhood fear of the dark resurfaces, and I rarely stray far from my tent.

Nevertheless, I try to think of the winds as celestial music, as a sacred gift. They sculpted these dunes. They bring the rain and snow that nourish the grasses. They generate the lightning that produces cleansing fire. At night they rattle us from sleep, reminding us that we are enveloped in creative energy and that our home planet is spinning toward eternity.

Everyone who lives in the Sandhills achieves some kind of accommodation with the winds. A rancher from Hyannis told me, "Most of the time you get used to it, but sometimes it kind of wears you down." A more typical Sandhills reaction came from a friend who lives in Alliance. As we stood by the roadside, barely able to hear one another over the roar of a July gale, I asked if he ever found the summer winds dispiriting. "Not really," he said. "Sometimes we get a little breeze, like today. It keeps the mosquitoes away."

Nineteenth-century explorers wrote in awe about the violent weather they encountered in the Sandhills. Dr. Thomas Maghee, who traveled up the Dismal and Niobrara River canyons with a military scouting expedition in 1873, scribbled this near-hysterical account of a Sandhills thunderstorm: "Ye Gods what a storm Wind like lightning tornado rain in torrents lightning in sheets. Thunder that shakes the earth hail stones three inches long in one continuous storm like bullets from a Gatling battery. Tents all down bedding scattered to the extent of vision Horses & mules stampeded Officers issuing orders or crouching under wagons Men cursing running all confusion. I'm out of breath."

During the early days of white settlement, the winds chased many people back east and drove others crazy. A young housewife living along Pine Creek during the 1880s had complained about the wind and drought for months. One day neighbors found her hanging from a rafter of her dugout home. A 1915 tornado that struck near Oshkosh reduced James Blair's house to splinters scattered over three miles of prairie. Friends recovered his mangled body from a grassy swale half a mile east of where the house had stood.

Nebraska local histories overflow with tales of killer storms. No one will ever forget the blizzard of 1949, when forty-foot drifts blocked rural roads for six weeks, or the winter of 1936, when horses sank belly deep in snow and temperatures stayed below zero for a month. But one blizzard has achieved legendary status throughout the state. Known as the "schoolchildren's storm of 1888," it exemplifies the deadly fury of suddenly shifting winds.

January 12, 1888, dawned warm and clear. Men in shirtsleeves worked in the fields, and schoolchildren played outdoors on the bare, frost-free ground. About noon a cold breeze eased in from the north, and the temperature began to fall. A fine, powdery snow floated down. By 2 P.M. the thermometer at Valentine had plummeted to −6 degrees Fahrenheit and wind gusts exceeded fifty miles an hour.

H. E. Clements, who was at home in his three-room sod house south of Hay Springs when the storm hit, described its fury in his reminiscences written sixty-seven years later: "The storm came down upon us from the northwest like a pack of mountain lions on a flock of sheep. We succeeded in getting our chores completed and the stock fed on the eve of January 12, but from that night on it was not safe to venture more than a few feet from the house for nearly three days. The air was filled with floury snow and the whirling wind was so intense, one could not breathe more than a few seconds without returning to the house."

Throughout Nebraska, schoolchildren were preparing to leave for home when the storm hit. The teachers' efforts to save the children have coalesced into one of Nebraska's most enduring memories.

Lois May Royce was teaching a class of nine pupils in a one-room schoolhouse near Plainview. Six of the children went home at noon, leaving her with Peter Poggensee, age nine, Otto Rosburg, nine, and Hattie Rosburg, six. When they realized there wasn't enough fuel in the schoolhouse to keep them warm through the night, Lois and the three children headed out into the storm, hoping to reach her room in a farmhouse two hundred yards to the north. They got lost and wandered about in a howling whiteout for several hours before huddling together, exhausted, in a depression at the base of a small haystack. At dawn Lois left the children's lifeless bodies and crawled on numb hands and knees to a neighbor's house. She survived but lost both her feet and the use of one hand.

In Dodge County two girls aged thirteen and seven begged their teacher to excuse them early so they could rush home to their widowed mother. Several days later rescuers dug their corpses out of a huge snowdrift. The seven-year-old was bundled up in her older sister's coat.

At the Midvale school near Ord, in the North Loup River Valley, seventeen-year-old Minnie May Freeman decided to keep her sixteen pupils at school for the night. But the wind blew down the door and began to rip off the roof.

Fine snow swirled around the classroom and drifted against the south wall.

Minnie consulted the oldest pupils, and they decided to try to make it to her boarding place half a mile away. Tied together by a lariat, the teacher and sixteen pupils staggered out into the storm.

All made it to safety, suffering only minor frostbite. Newspapers across the country published greatly exaggerated accounts of their trek, and Minnie Freeman became a regional hero whose exploits are still recounted to children throughout Nebraska.

Across the state somewhere between two hundred and a thousand people perished in the "schoolchildren's storm." At the Clements place the family holed up for three days as the temperature plunged to -35 degrees Fahrenheit. When they finally emerged, they found drifts piled higher than the rooftops and the barn so full of snow that the horses and mules were "almost standing on their heads," wedged up against the rafters.

SHIFTING SANDS

Nothing lives long,
Only the Earth and the Mountains.

—White Antelope, Cheyenne Chief

WHEN JULES Sandoz came to the Sand-hills in 1884, he quickly learned how to find his way home during a blizzard. Lakota friends told him to find a blowout. These conspicuous, wind-carved craters tend to open out toward the southeast, away from the strongest winds. Lost travelers walked from blowout to blowout, using them as a compass.

If you fly over the Sandhills, you can clearly see the sweep of the dunes, generally from northwest to southeast, like waves rippling across the plains or folds in an enormous dress spread out over the earth. Fierce winds molded these dunes from sand deposited over millions of years by rivers flowing down from the Rocky Mountains to the west.

For a long time scientists thought the dunes must have formed 12,000 to 20,000 years ago, during the Wisconsin glaciation, when loess (fine particles of windblown silt) accumulated in adjacent regions of Nebraska. During the 1970s geologists began to drill test holes through the sand, searching for organic material that could be carbon-dated. Near the base of one dune they found organic material that was only 1,500 years old. Other test holes yielded material between 5,000 and 13,000 years old. The oldest date corresponds with the end of the last ice age, when the Great Plains climate became warmer and drier. The dunes we see today probably began forming as the glaciers retreated, and dunes continued to form sporadically, during relatively dry periods, until very recent times.

Scientists believe dunes can form and move only when vegetation cover falls below about 30 percent. This could have happened in western Nebraska when annual precipitation averaged less than ten inches, about 50 percent of current levels. Fire frequency and strength of prevailing winds also influence dune movement.

The dunes come in many shapes and sizes. There are narrow linear dunes, squat domelike dunes, and U-shaped parabolic dunes. Large crescent-shaped dunes, known as barchans, form where the wind molds horn-shaped ridges on the lee side of the dune crest.

In the north-central Sandhills, the barchans flow together to form long elephant-backed ridges known as barchanoid-ridge dunes. These immense ridges of sand, some four hundred feet high and ten miles long, stretch from west to east across the landscape. Between them lie flat, narrow valleys where bobolinks and savannah sparrows chatter in wet meadows and beavers build their lodges along meandering brooks. These isolated valleys may hold the key to understanding both the recent geologic history of the Sandhills and their future.

During a hot, dry autumn more than sixty years ago, a northern Cherry County rancher noticed that one of his meadows was on fire. He found a hay bale that had been ignited by lightning. Smoke and steam rose from the surrounding soil. He could not put out the fire, and the meadow smoldered for more than a month.

Experiences like this one, along with 1930s soil surveys, alerted scientists to peat in the interdunal valleys. The peat, a mat of compressed vegetation, occurs in saturated meadows where the constant presence of groundwater at the soil surface slows decomposition of organic matter. Sandhills peat feels and smells like the peat that Irish farmers have dug up and used as fuel for centuries. But Irish peat typically comes from bogs that are fed by abundant precipitation. Since Sandhills peatlands are maintained by groundwater flow, they are classified as fens.

Finding fens on the plains is like discovering glaciers in the tropics. The central Sandhills receive only twenty inches of precipitation a year, and evaporation is far greater. Strangely, the arid climate may help form these wetlands. Geologists believe the saturated meadows between the ridges may have been created when dune movement during dry periods dammed up natural drainages. The massive reservoir of groundwater that mounds up beneath the dunes provides continuous moisture to the fens.

Peatlands in a semiarid landscape are remarkable enough, but the surface vegetation of Sandhills fens is astonishing. Cotton grass, an eighteen-inch-high sedge usually found in cold northern environments, thrives there, along with marsh marigold, bog aster, wild lily, and sensitive fern. This plant community, likely a relict of the Ice Age, suggests that the fens have existed for at least 12,000 years. Radiocarbon dating of lower peat layers confirms this theory.

Puffs of cotton grass seed nod in the evening breeze as geologist Jim Swinehart and I slosh through the Jumbo Valley fen, a Nature Conservancy property sixty miles southwest of Valentine. The ground quakes under our feet like a giant trampoline and rises gently as we move toward the center of the fen, where the peat has sucked up groundwater like a sponge, creating its own topography. Jim twists his hand auger down into the muck. He removes a three-foot core of peat, an eight-inch layer of fine, wet sand, then another layer of peat. The peat immediately above this sand layer has been radiocarbon-dated at about 800 years before the present. The peat below the sand layer dates back about 900 years. Not too long ago, at about the time the Anasazi civilization was flourishing in the American Southwest and William the Conqueror ruled England, sheets of sand were blowing across this valley.

Deep cores drilled through the peat reveal several sand layers. Radiocarbon dates above and below the thickest layer correspond with the "altithermal" period, 5,000 to 8,000 years ago, when a hot, dry climate prevailed on the plains.

Jim and his colleagues at the University of Nebraska first began studying Sandhills fens during the early 1990s. "We had been aware of the fens," he says, "but we didn't realize the treasure they held in terms of a climate record with eolian [windblown] sand interbedded with peat. They give us the chance to compile a stream of radiocarbon dates going back 12,000 years or more."

The geologists have found 12,000-year-old peat under some of the higher dunes adjacent to the fens. They hope eventually to drill enough cores to track dune movement across the landscape and to confirm that episodes of sand movement were synchronous in time throughout the Sandhills.

They also have discovered 12,000-year-old streambeds that have been buried and blocked by shifting sands. Crescent Lake was created when an enormous "sand dam" blocked the flow of Blue Creek about 5,000 years ago. The two-mile-long lake is gradually filling up with muck and peat, and lake water will eventually overflow the sand dam, reopening the ancient valley. The Jumbo Valley fen also occupies what appears to be a blocked stream drainage.

While a flock of barn swallows swoops over the canary grass and willow thickets, Jim talks about the sense of movement in this landscape. "The gut feeling I had when we started working in the Sandhills was that this is a young landscape. Now we're confirming that the Holocene [the period since the last ice age] was a period of intense activity. And we have these plants living out there, the cotton grass as a kind of a symbol of how resilient certain microsystems can be. I mean, this place was abused in the mid-Holocene, but they hung on."

Across the valley a dune one hundred feet high stands slightly apart from the others, just beyond the margin of the fen. We imagine this dune, mostly barren of vegetation, drifting across the valley 5,000 to 8,000 years ago while the cotton grass continued to bloom in an island of peat. This image, a contrast of metamorphosis and stasis, challenges human intuition. But we know that something of that nature happened here, and we know it will happen again.

IT SEEMS ironic that one of North America's best preserved landscapes is also among its youngest. The feeling of timelessness that visitors to the region experience is misleading. In fifty years, relatively little has changed; in 12,000 years, a lot has changed. Should a prolonged dry period set in, an eventuality predicted by many scientists studying global warming, today's lush prairie could vanish in less than a lifetime.

By existing, the Sandhills prairie foretells its own demise. The prairie is a creature of the dunes, and dunes of this type can form only when the sand is largely barren of vegetation. With or without global warming, the cycle of greening and drifting will continue.

At the same time, the Sandhills are relatively drought-proof. The picture of periodic sand movement that is emerging from research in the fens indicates that some areas remained wet and green during times when the dunes were barren and drifting. Scientists have found bison tracks within a variety of dune strata and have uncovered the remains of prehistoric hunting and fishing camps near Sandhills wetlands. During droughts, the relatively moist Sandhills valleys, nourished by the underlying aquifer, provided a refuge for plants and animals. The grass receded, the dunes shifted, but the hills greened up again when the rains returned.

Over the longer haul, this resilience will be even more severely tested. Analysis of ice cores from glaciers in Greenland and Antarctica shows that the climate of the Holocene has been remarkably stable. Scientists have noted several periods during the previous half-million years when mean global temperatures appear to have risen or fallen as much as 10 degrees Fahrenheit, sometimes within a few decades. No one is sure of the cause of these climatic gyrations; they could result from reconfiguration of ocean currents, volcanic eruptions, or sudden melting of polar ice. But it's doubtful that this relatively mild spell we're experiencing will last forever. Some atmospheric scientists believe our ongoing pollution of the atmosphere with greenhouse gases could trigger a climatic perturbation similar to those that occurred before the Holocene.

One way or another, we'll have to get used to the idea that the natural ecosystems we strive so hard to protect and restore are subject to sudden metamorphosis. Whenever we plan to restore an ecosystem to its natural state, we probably should ask, Natural during what time period? We know that 6,000 years ago this prairie was mostly sand desert; 6,000 years from now it may be something entirely different from either prairie or desert.

Does this realization imply that we should love natural ecosystems any less? For my part, the more aware I become of the fragility and impermanence of this prairie, the more urgently I need to feel its textures and inhale its beauty.

The most stable of landforms experience constant erosion, and these dunes shift slightly even during the relatively wet periods. I appreciate this reality whenever I watch tiny rivulets form on the steep sides of a blowout during a spring downpour or stand out in the open when an early summer cold front roars through. It's mostly illusion, but when the wind blows hard enough to affect your balance and mental stability, the topography seems as alive as the grasses and wildlife.

One hot afternoon in early June I sit propped against a ponderosa at Pine Lake, south of Rushville, reading and photographing the occasional pelican flock that floats by. A soft breeze comes up out of the north, setting the pine boughs in motion and sending cool ripples across the water.

As I rise and stretch, the breeze picks up. The pines creak and moan, a blizzard of fluffy cottonwood seed fills the air, and tears begin to stream down my wind-battered face. I watch transfixed as the mercury on my portable thermometer drops from 92 to 53 degrees in ten minutes.

My tent. I glimpse the blue gray dome as it shoots between a pair of ponderosas like a giant football sailing through the uprights. It bounces up a low hill, gains altitude, and flies off toward Kansas.

The tent and I skip across the dunes, swept along by the gale and obscured by the cottonwood snow, like characters in an Italian neorealist film. I cast furtive glances over my shoulder, hoping no one's watching. An unnecessary precaution. No humans are in sight, and even the cows have run for cover. The lake surface froths with white foam as the wind lashes the young cottonwoods along the lakeshore, bending them nearly to the ground.

Finally the tent tumbles into a depression and deflates as I wrestle it into submission. I fight my way back to camp with it swirling behind me like a great blue kite.

Out over the hills the sky has changed color, from clear blue to gritty rose gray. Somewhere nearby the sands are shifting and the landscape is subtly transforming before the capricious blasts of the northwest wind.

PAWNEE SPRINGS

I do not want to leave this place. God gave us these lands.

—Terrecowah, Pawnee chief

IN SOME places the Loup River's waters run so clear that they magnify the crystalline sand on the river bottom. Seen from a highway bridge or an embankment, the white sand dances and swirls hypnotically in the rolling current. In other places, where the Loup flows more swiftly or bubbles up from deep artesian springs, the water and sand mix into a thick gray soup. Some of the springs are several feet across and go down more than one hundred feet, right into the heart of the High Plains aquifer.

This aquifer, one of the largest groundwater resources in North America, stretches from Nebraska to Texas, but it is deepest under the Sandhills. Precipitation falling on the hills percolates down into a complex of sands, sandstones, and gravels one hundred to nine hundred feet thick overlying a deeper layer of impermeable sandstones. Like a giant sponge, the Sandhills and the underlying aggregate collect snow and rainwater and then release it slowly through the thousands of springs that feed the region's lakes and streams. So much water is trapped close to the surface that the Loup and other Sandhills rivers recharge at a nearly constant rate. The Loup carries almost as much water in October as in June.

The Pawnee told stories about the people who lived down there, in the fountain of life under the river. The turtle people could transform themselves back and forth from human to animal. The Nahu'rac, an animal clan of bears, mountain lions, bison, elk, beavers, otters, deer, and many kinds of birds, dwelt in caverns under the river. The Nahu'rac's messenger was the kingfisher, who flew swiftly over the water and could dive straight into their underground lodges.

One story, recounted by George Grinnell in *Pawnee, Blackfoot, and Cheyenne*, tells of a man who sacrificed his son to the creator, Tira'wa, believing this act would bring him blessings and wisdom. The man stabbed his son with a long knife and threw him into the river. The body floated down until it came to the great whirlpool that is the entrance to one of the lodges of the Nahu'rac. Two vultures lifted the boy's body out of the water and laid it on top of the bluff above the river. The kingfisher flew to the Nahu'rac, telling them of the boy's plight and asking them to restore him to life.

The Nahu'rac revived the boy and taught him all their secrets, including how to cut a man open and cure him, how to shoot an arrow through a man without hurting him, and how to bring the dead back to life. After the boy returned to his people, he became a great healer, and the secrets he had learned from the Nahu'rac were passed along to many generations of Pawnee healers.

Some of the first whites to visit the Pawnee saw these healing acts and concluded that the Pawnee shamans had supernatural powers. Ethnographers say most of the Pawnee knew that the healing acts were only illusions but still believed that anyone who could perform such clever tricks must be wise and powerful.

I like to read about the Pawnee mythology while lying in the soft green grass along the middle fork of the Loup River, near Halsey. The stories, filled with magic and reverence for nature, capture the flavor of this country of fertile valleys and immense, turbulent skies. These same stories circulated around the vicinity of my campfire pit throughout the eighteenth and early nineteenth centuries, when the names *Loup* and *Pawnee* became nearly synonymous.

The Republican, Platte, and Loup River Valleys sustained the Pawnee people for more than two hundred years. French trappers named the Loup (Wolf) River after one of the four main Pawnee bands, the Skiri, or Wolf Pawnee.

According to Pawnee oral tradition, the name Skiri originally referred to a small band of Pawnee who lived along a
stretch of river where wolves gathered to feed on the carcasses of bison stranded on the ice.

Over time the Skiri were said to have taken on the at-
tributes of wolves. Skiri warriors disguised themselves as
wolves to sneak up on the enemy, and the nocturnal wolf
howls of Skiri scouts passed for the real thing. Grinnell reported that Pawnee scouts also had the endurance of
wolves. He said runners typically traveled one hundred
miles in twenty-four hours, and he cited an instance when
two Pawnee men ran seventy miles in only twelve hours.

The Skiri referred to the river not as the Loup but as the
Its-kari, "potatoes many," after the ground nuts that flourished along its banks. The Skiri dug up these small tubers
along with wild licorice, bush morning glory roots,
Jerusalem artichokes, prairie turnips, and wild onions; they
picked chokecherries, elderberries, prickly pears, wild plums,
and sand cherries; and they gathered fresh greens of bee
balm, common milkweed, and lamb's-quarter. They planted
fields of corn, beans, and squash each spring and harvested
them each fall. In late summer and again in late fall, the
Skiri dispersed southward toward the Republican River and
westward into the Sandhills to hunt bison, elk, deer,
beavers, and other wild game.

The three forks of the Loup River, originating in the
eastern half of the Sandhills, flow through narrow, sparsely
wooded valleys, green and fertile at the bottom, sandy and

windswept at the top. The country's mood changes from moment to moment. In winter balmy, blue-sky days may portend raging blizzards. In summer fresh, dewy mornings give way to hazy, stifling afternoons. Evening thunderstorms strike violently and recede quickly, revealing a night sky inky black and awash with stars.

The Pawnee attributed their origins to these stars, and they planned daily and seasonal activities to harmonize with the rhythms of the heavens. They laid their villages out in the patterns of familiar constellations. They aligned their hemispherical houses with the celestial sphere; the entryway faced east, toward the morning star, and an altar on the far wall faced west, toward the evening star. Openings in the roof permitted the elders to view the positions of the stars, the planets, the sun, and the moon. Overhead and in every direction was Tira'wa, the Creator. In the beginning, he instructed the morning and evening stars to mate, producing the first Pawnee woman, and he bade the sun and moon to do the same, creating the first Pawnee man. When Pawnee men and women died, they returned to the heavens as stars.

The Pawnee roundhouse represented both the universe and the womb. The women's beds were arranged within the lodge according to the stages of a woman's life. The youngest women slept in the deepest part of the womb, the garden of the evening star. The older women slept near the entrance/exit, the pathway to the "outside." The word for house was *a-ka-ru*, "inside place"; the word for universe was *ka-huraru*, "the inside land."

Each morning before dawn, Pawnee elders stepped outside to study the stars' positions and plan the coming day. The Pawnee worshiped dawn as a time of creation and wonder. Tahirussawichi, a Pawnee shaman, described the coming of dawn in *American Indian Poetry*, by George Cronyn:

> As we sing the morning star comes nearer, moving swiftly toward its birthplace. . . . We call to Mother Earth, who is represented by the ear of corn. She has been asleep and resting during the night. We ask her to awake, to move, to arise, for the signs of dawn are seen in the east and the breath of new life is here.
>
> Mother Earth hears the call; she moves, she awakes, she arises, she feels the warmth of the new-born Dawn. The leaves and the grass stir; all things move with the breath of the new day; everywhere life is renewed.
>
> This is very mysterious; we are speaking of something very sacred, although it happens every day.

Before the spring planting, the fall harvest, and the spring and winter bison hunts, the Pawnee conducted lengthy creation and awakening ceremonies, interacting with Tira'wa and the star gods to elicit cosmic unity and fruitfulness. The Skiri chief Petalesharo explained these ways to an Indian agent in 1872: "Before we go on a hunt, before we plant, we make a feast and old men sing and Tira'wa lets things grow. When corn gets so high, we have a ceremony and ask God to give us it to live and get Buffalo. We offer our food to God before eating. I like this way and don't want to lose it."

The Pawnee timed important events by observing the positions of the constellations. The Pawnee year began in early spring when two stars known as the Swimming Ducks (probably two bright stars in Scorpio) appeared above the eastern horizon and the Pleiades, or Seven Sisters, descended in the west. These stars instructed the animals to awaken from their winter's sleep, break through the ice, and come up from the underground. Elders listened for the first thunder of the year, the voice of the creative force, Tira'wa. Once the thunder rumbled, priests could perform the spring renewal ceremonies that would help bring the world back to life. For the Pawnee life was a continuous, rhythmic dance with their creators, the stars.

Yet Pawnee life was far from idyllic. Hard winters left some people starving and frostbitten. Warfare became an accepted part of existence during the eighteenth and nineteenth centuries as displaced groups from the north and east pressed in on Pawnee lands. Battles with the Sicangu and Oglala Lakota grew particularly frequent and bloody. (Sicangu is the Lakota name for the tribe also known as the Brulé [French for "burnt thighs"] or the Rosebud Sioux.) Lakota warriors ambushed a Pawnee hunting party near the Republican River on August 5, 1873, and killed at least sixty-nine Pawnee. The Pawnee leader Tirawahut Resaru, already mourning the loss of a wife and two daughters in a previous Lakota raid, reputedly stabbed his three-year-old son in the heart to prevent him from falling into enemy hands.

Daily life, marked by love and respect among families and reverence for the powers above, also included acts of perplexing cruelty. Until the early nineteenth century, the Skiri practiced a ritual known as the captive girl sacrifice. A young captive from another tribe was kept in a special lodge, where she was dressed in the finest clothes and fed special foods. Then she was lashed to a post and brutally slaughtered with spears and arrows. Village women and children watched gleefully as Skiri warriors scooped up handfuls of the captive's warm blood to smear on their faces. Eagle Chief, an old Pawnee who had witnessed the ceremony during the early 1800s, spoke of its significance in *The Lost Universe*, by Gene Weltfish: "The man who had killed the captive fasted and mourned for four days and asked Tira'wa to take pity on him, for he knew he had taken the life of a human being. . . . this sacrifice always seemed acceptable to Tira'wa, and when the Skiri made it, they always seemed to have good fortune in war, and good crops, and they were always well."

MY TENT sits in a grove of ponderosa pines planted during the early 1900s, when the federal government decided to create a Nebraska National Forest. The "forest," really an open woodland, extends half a dozen miles to the south, most of the way to the Dismal River canyon. From my picnic table I can hear a cardinal whistling in the box elders beside the Middle Loup and children shouting and splashing in the water.

The river here is about fifty yards across, thigh deep, and swift enough to carry a canoe along at three miles an hour. A set of railway tracks parallels the north shore. At half-hour intervals, long freight trains rumble by loaded with coal from eastern Wyoming's Thunder Basin.

At night when I go walking along the river, the trains fade into the background and the valley begins to feel wild and peaceful. One evening just before sunset I discover a place where water trickles from a steep embankment overgrown with green ash, chokecherry, nettles, and trailing vines of wild grape and clematis. A giant cottonwood stands guard over the shallow green pool where the springwater collects before seeping down into the river. Golden monkey flowers nod above the algae-encrusted shore, where bright yellow swallowtails and midnight blue damselflies flit through a dying shaft of sunlight.

My approach prompts a dozen baby bullfrogs to splash across the pond and sink eye-deep into the camouflaging ooze of moss and algae. A painted turtle scurries from its perch atop a half-submerged log and plops into the water. Suddenly the ground gives way, and I find myself standing in an eighteen-inch-deep tunnel dug by beavers commuting from the river to the spring. Multilayered tracks of white-tailed deer, raccoons, and opposums cover every square inch of shoreline.

Many years ago, when the Pawnee were very poor and there were no bison to hunt, a young man came to a spring like this one to pray and cry out for a vision. He became entranced by the moon's reflection in the water. When he swam over that way, he saw the face of an old woman. She told him to go up on the highest hill above the spring and cry out.

The young man spent the night and most of the next day on the hill, crying out and praying. That evening he returned to the spring to drink. As he knelt beside the water, he looked into the cave where the spring burst forth and saw a young girl sitting there. He bowed his head to drink again. When he looked up, he saw a mature woman sitting in the cave. He bent to drink a third time. When he looked up he saw a middle-aged woman. After he drank a fourth time, he gazed into the cave and saw the old woman he had talked to the night before.

The old woman led him into the cave. Inside was another world, filled with wondrous things. In the various directions, he saw the faces of the four women. The young girl stood near the entrance, to the west. The mature woman stood inside to the southwest. The middle-aged woman stood to the southeast. The old woman stood deep in the cave, to the east. When he looked her way, she vanished.

A high, clear voice echoed from the cave entrance.

"Now do you know me?" the young woman asked. "No," the man answered.

"I am the new moon," she said. "The old woman you saw was the moon become old. She disappears, and I come again as a girl. Walk outside with me and we will talk."

As they emerged from the cave, the girl transformed into the old woman. She sat down beside the man and told a story. "Your people are poor," she said, "but I have gifts for you." She gave him some special sticks, a ring, and a basket of plum seeds, all for the people to play with so they would forget their hunger. Later, she instructed him in the proper way to build earth lodges, to hunt bison, and to plant and harvest corn.

The games Mother Moon had given the people distracted them from their hunger until it was time for the bison to appear. Finally, as the people were growing restless from waiting, the bison burst forth from the cave and spread out across the prairie. The people hunted the bison and planted corn and had plenty to eat from that time on.

When the young man returned to the cave, he found that the spring was dry and the cave entrance had disappeared. After the people heard that the magic of the place was gone, they broke up into bands and scattered over the prairie.

I sit by the spring until the moonlight begins to filter through the trees and the droning of cicadas ebbs away and returns as a soothing chorus of crickets. A bullfrog croaks in the night shadow beyond the pond, and a spotted sandpiper whistles in triplets down along the river. The moon's face looks small and lifeless in the murky water. The only animal form I see is the feathery white image of a barn-owl, captured where a moonbeam illuminates the knobby trunk of the old cottonwood.

THE CLEAR, flowing springs of the North, Middle, and South Loup Rivers enticed European American explorers into the region during the early nineteenth century. The Pawnee signed their first treaty of friendship with the whites in 1818. Four years later Skiri chief Petalesharo traveled to Washington to inform President Monroe that his people wanted to be left alone. He spoke these prophetic words:

> We have plenty of buffalo, beaver, deer and other wild animals—we have an abundance of horses—we have everything we want—we have plenty of land, if you will keep your people off it.
>
> We are not starving yet—we wish you to permit us to enjoy the chase until the game of our country is exhausted—until the wild animals become extinct.

As the whites crowded in, capitulation became inevitable. In 1833 the four Pawnee bands gave up 13 million acres south of the Platte River in exchange for $4,600 in goods to be paid annually for twelve years. In 1848 they relinquished 110,000 acres north of the Platte in exchange for $2,000 in goods. In 1857 they turned over most of their remaining lands, about 10 million acres north of the Platte, for 21.7¢ an acre.

The promised annuities rarely came. Grasshoppers devoured the crops that Indian agents had advised the Pawnee to plant. Smallpox and other imported diseases decimated the population, reducing it from about ten thousand in 1830 to fewer than two thousand in 1874. Pawnee villages became, in the words of historian David Wishart, "open graveyards where the dogs were left to dispose of the bodies." In addition, the depleted villages became virtually defenseless against repeated raids by the well-armed Lakota. Finally, in 1874 the Pawnee gave up the rest of their land in Nebraska and trudged south to "Indian country" in Oklahoma.

Some of the chiefs left without complaint, realizing they had been completely boxed in by what George Bird Grinnell referred to as "a carefully planned and successfully carried out conspiracy to rob [them] of their lands." Others objected to the end. Lone Chief, of the Skiri, said, "I've made up my mind to stay here on my land. I am not going where I have nothing."

Today the Loup River valleys are filled with the white faces of Hereford cattle and of third- and fourth-generation ranchers of northern European origin. There are white farmhouses, narrow-steepled churches, and sleepy towns with wide, empty streets and crumbling brick buildings.

But this still seems like Pawnee country. A century of physical separation can hardly break the spiritual and emotional ties that bound a people to this land. On my evening walks beside the river I feel their spirit energy in the yips and howls of coyotes, in the sweet fragrance of chokecherry and milkweed blossoms, in the river's swirling sand, in the faint shadows created by the light of the watchful stars.

GRASS

Grass no good upside down.

—Plains Indian admonition to white settlers

IN EARLY fall, when folks drive to the mountains to watch the aspens change to gold, I set out over the hills to experience the turning of the grasses. I wade through shoulder-high stands of claret-hued Indian grass, run my fingers through the silvery seed heads of sand bluestem, and nestle into soft clumps of golden switchgrass. I revel in the crunch of prairie cordgrass underfoot and the hiss of the wind in prairie sand reed. I rub side oats grama seeds between my palms to remove the chaff, put the seeds on my tongue, and taste sunlight.

When the turning grasses transform the dunes into a mosaic of burgundy, russet, and amber, the prairie reveals its true complexity. On a shady hillside, a wine-colored patch of big bluestem draws its life energy from an underground spring. On the sunbaked summit a rattlesnake basks among the flaxen stems of blue grama and sand dropseed. Down below, in a subirrigated meadow, a dark green swath of prairie cordgrass shelters garter snakes, meadow voles, and a sleeping red fox.

This prairie is best appreciated at ground level, where you can poke your fingers into meadow vole runs and watch big black crickets and dung beetles scurry through a forest of grass stems. Homesteader Grace Snyder wrote, "I found that when I lay flat and still on my stomach, my ear to the ground, I could hear the grass growing, all its little roots pushing and digging like everything. And if I held my breath, it even seemed that I could hear the very small sound that time itself made as it went by."

I begin my walk through autumn at dawn, from the south shore of Pine Lake. Down here by the water, things are hopping. Bullfrogs plop, muskrats splash, coots cackle, while an enormous flock of blackbirds wheels overhead and a short-eared owl courses over the nodding cordgrass.

If I listen carefully, I can hear the rustling and nibbling of dozens of meadow voles. These large-headed, mouse-sized rodents are hard at work converting the sunlight stored in the cordgrass and switchgrass into flesh, fur, and bone. Their narrow runs, tunneling through the matted grasses, honeycomb the marsh.

Here and there, under a small mound of shredded grass, a female suckles her young. Models of fecundity, the voles breed monthly. A female can produce dozens of offspring in a single summer. In a predator-free environment (surely a meadow vole's idea of utopia) a pair could engender more than a thousand children, grandchildren, and great-grandchildren in a single year.

Short-eared owls, marsh hawks, red-tailed hawks, American kestrels, mink, red foxes, and coyotes descend on the marsh to participate in this massive energy conversion. At each level of the food chain—from grass to vole to predator—about 90 percent of the available energy is given off as heat or returned to the soil. Thus it takes about one hundred pounds of grass to maintain ten pounds of vole to maintain one pound of hawk. If I had a scythe and a scale, I could estimate the number of predators in this marsh. From where I stand, up to my shoulders in switchgrass, I'm aware of two of them, a marsh hawk gliding over the cattails and a coyote yipping in the distance.

Voles and vole hunters aren't the only creatures that have benefited from the dense sod laid down by the moisture-loving cordgrass and switchgrass. Indians living on the eastern Great Plains used cordgrass for thatch, and during the homesteading years of the late nineteenth and early twentieth centuries, cordgrass and switchgrass became the walls and roofs of thousands of prairie homes. Settlers cut the sod into strips and laid them out to dry, and many hands were bloodied by the razor-sharp leaves of the cordgrass. Then they stacked the sod bricks to form walls, framed the door, windows, and roof with timber, and piled several layers of sod on top of the rafters. Sometimes they added a wooden floor and whitewashed the walls and ceiling. The dwellings they built were warm in winter, cool in summer, and leaked like crazy.

A typical sod house was a work in progress, usually beginning as one large room housing native flora and fauna along with the humans and a domestic animal or two. Rattlesnakes curled up between the sod blocks. Wildflowers unfurled on the roof. Walls reverberated with cricket song. Musty odors of drying earth, roots, and grass permeated every nook and cranny, blurring the demarcation between "inside" and "outside," between the artificial and the natural.

Most of us, except perhaps children who dig subterranean forts in the backyard, have forgotten the atavistic appeal of earth and sod. Today when you say the word "grass," people envision either groomed lawns or marijuana. But somewhere deep in our genetic memory lie soothing recollections of the coarse textures and pungent organic aromas that once bound many of our ancestors to the earth. A roll in the switchgrass on a frosty October morning is all it takes to bring these feelings flooding back.

White-tailed deer also love to bed down in switch-grass, so I'm more gratified than surprised when a young buck springs up and sprints over the nearest hill. I follow, leaving the wetlands behind. The cordgrass disappears, the switchgrass patches become smaller and more scattered, and walking gets easier. Here, in the gentle uplands around the lake, the dominant grasses grow only about waist high.

The most conspicuous are prairie sand reed, two to three feet high with a full, arrow-shaped panicle of small, hairy seeds, and sand bluestem, tall and erect with feathery seed heads that glow in the morning sunlight. Scattered among these dominants are big bluestem, little bluestem, Indian ricegrass, sand dropseed, porcupine grass, and a dozen other species. Root systems that extend ten feet or more under the sandy soil let these upland grasses absorb the moisture that trickles down through the dunes. Neighboring yucca plants have taproots up to five feet long and a foot thick, and their lateral roots may extend ten feet down and twenty-five feet horizontally.

The big bluestem, easily identified by its three-pronged "turkey foot" seed heads, is the same grass that stood "taller than a man on horseback" in the tallgrass prairies of the Mississippi and Missouri Valleys. Cattle and people could get lost in the sea of grass seven to ten feet high. In the Sandhills, big bluestem grows only in small four- to six-foot-high patches on moist sites. Its shorter cousin, little bluestem, grows in bunches on drier hillsides. Both display a palette of colors on every stem, grading from blue-green to maroon and burnt sienna.

As I walk through this upland prairie, grasshopper sparrows flit from one patch of tall grass to the next. A meadowlark, either confused by the day length or rehearsing for next year, warbles a truncated territorial song. Two sharp-tailed grouse flush and fly off into the rising sun. Shotguns rumble in the distance.

I climb to the top of the highest dune and sit in a small blowout. Here the grama grass, sand dropseed, blowout grass, and sand bluestem grow in widely scattered clumps. Ragged patches of pasture sage and sand cherry cling to a wind-buffeted ridge. No birds sing. Only a few insect and mammal tracks ornament the exposed sand. The revelry of the marshes and lowland prairies seems a world away.

I SIT FOR an hour waiting for something to come by. All I see are grasshoppers. Little green ones cling to the underside of the most succulent stems. Big red and yellow ones spring through the air. Others take flight with a loud buzz like a rattlesnake. Grasshoppers. The word adds a hint of foreboding to the most serene of situations.

In Rushville and Purdum, Oshkosh and Alliance, summer and early fall conversation often turns to grasshoppers. How bad are they this year? How much of your garden did they eat? Grasshoppers, as much as bison, pronghorn, and prairie dogs, symbolize the North American prairie. If this country was made for anything, it was made for grasshoppers.

There are more species of grasshoppers in Nebraska than there are of mammals. A couple of hundred varieties hop through the state's grasslands, farmlands, and woodlands. Grasshoppers predate humans by close to 200 million years, and they'll no doubt thrive long after we're extinct.

Grasshopper populations can explode without warning. Nymphs hatch from eggs as miniature, wingless versions of their parents. They begin hopping and eating immediately. Within a few weeks they're ready to fly. Females can lay several hundred eggs, which are buried an inch or so down in the soil, primed to hatch during the first warm days of spring. During the High Plains grasshopper infestation of 1958, biologists counted as many as six hundred grasshoppers emerging from a square yard of soil.

By all appearances the Rocky Mountain locust, *Melanoplus spretus*, was just another grasshopper. But for reasons not fully understood by scientists, it had a unique life history. When conditions were just right—possibly a succession of mild autumns followed by cool, wet springs—populations multiplied exponentially until these locusts (a term that means simply "migratory grasshopper") gathered into immense swarms near the foot of the Rockies and sailed eastward in dark clouds of destruction.

The most devastating outbreaks occurred between 1874 and 1877. During the summer of 1874, crackling clouds of locusts descended on prairie farms, devouring everything in sight. Grasshoppers dropped from the sky like hailstones. In places they covered the ground four inches deep. They ate all the crops and then went to work on trees, fences, window curtains, kitchen utensils, and furniture. Farmers came after them with gunny sacks, water, and fire. Nothing stemmed the tide. One Nebraska settler recalled watching helplessly as an army of locusts chewed away every bit of the green stripe on her white dress.

In *Sod and Stubble*, John Ise describes a typical invasion: "Like a cloud of glistening snow flakes it was, but the flakes were alive, eddying and whirling about like the wild, dead leaves in an autumn storm; and soon the flakes came down, circling in myriads, beating against everything animate or inanimate. Grasshoppers—millions, billions of them— soon covered the ground in a seething, fluttering mass, their jaws constantly at work."

Observers in Nebraska estimated the size of one swarm at nearly a mile high, one hundred miles across, and three hundred miles deep. The swarm, thought to contain more than 100 billion locusts, moved eastward at about five miles an hour.

After 1877 the locust outbreaks became less severe. Within a few decades *Melanoplus spretus* seems to have disappeared completely. No one knows why. Perhaps conditions changed on the grasshoppers' Rocky Mountain breeding grounds. Perhaps more sedentary grasshoppers began to outcompete this mercurial species. But though locust outbreaks of biblical magnitude have not occurred on the Great Plains for more than a hundred years, some residents wonder if the Rocky Mountain locust is really extinct or is still lurking out there somewhere.

The great locust outbreaks struck as the first cattle ranches were being established on the edge of the Sandhills. Ranchers must have watched in horror as the great swarms swept through, devouring almost everything green. But the grass recovered quickly.

Nevertheless, the Sandhills region continued to experience ripple effects from the locust invasions for several years as westering settlers, some wiped out by the plagues of 1874 to 1877, homesteaded marginal lands near the Niobrara and Loup Rivers. These settlers would discover a different kind of plague, with more enduring consequences. It was called cultivation.

"THE RAIN will follow the plow." So said the promotional pamphlets distributed by land speculators and railroad developers hoping to lure homesteaders to the arid prairie. The theory held that once the soil was turned and crops were planted, ambient humidity would increase, changing the climate.

Nebraska promoter C. D. Wilber pushed descriptive language to its most florid extremes in describing the climatic transformation that would result from turning the soil: "In this miracle of progress, the plow is the avant courier—the unerring prophet—the procuring cause. Not by any magic or enchantment, nor by incantations or offerings but instead in the sweat of his face, toiling with his hands, man can persuade the heavens to yield their treasures of dew and rain upon the land he has chosen for a dwelling place."

Wilber's sidekick in the prairie promotion business, biology professor Samuel Aughey, predicted that as agriculture marched inexorably westward, Nebraska's climate would begin to approach the "wonderful conditions of the Tertiary epoch . . . [when] magnificent forests reared themselves on the borders of lakes [and] this section of country must have enjoyed the delightful climate and balmy breezes we now associate with Mexico and Cuba."

Aughey added with questionable logic that if rain followed the plow it would also follow telegraph lines, roads, towns, fences, railroad tracks, and irrigation ditches. Even the Sandhills, he exulted in 1880, would "someday be cultivated." Once cultivated, the area would become a veritable Garden of Eden as precipitation increased steadily from year to year. Between 1865 and 1885, prairie promoters like Wilber and Aughey contributed their theories to millions of promotional pamphlets that were distributed throughout the United States and Europe.

The prospect of free land in a potential paradise west of the one hundredth meridian must have seemed irresistible to poor, landless farmers. Many headed west without any understanding of what they were getting into. Some were lured there by disillusioned relatives and friends who, after migrating, realized they would need reinforcements to survive in the arid wilderness.

For newlyweds Gideon and Margaret Waggoner of Sullivan County, Indiana, heading west may have seemed the only option. Margaret's parents had lost all their savings during a financial panic, and Gideon had little money. After spending their first married winter living with Margaret's parents, the young couple managed to scrape together enough money to join a westering expedition led by the Rev. John A. Scamahorn.

A born-again Methodist and a Civil War veteran, Scamahorn was a powerful preacher with a devoted following. Health problems and the urging of a friend in the land-promotion business persuaded him, at age fifty-three, to move his family and a sizable number of his flock west to Nebraska, "the Paradise of the West."

On March 20, 1884, Scamahorn departed by train for Valentine with a colony of 104 settlers, including Margaret and Gideon Waggoner. At Valentine, Margaret and Gideon unloaded their wagon, team of oxen, two cows, some secondhand furniture, and various provisions, and the group set out across country for Gordon. Along the way they encountered a tornado that nearly blew away their tent and a prairie fire that scorched miles of grassland.

One day some members of the party stopped at a little sod house to see if they could buy feed for their cows and oxen. A woman came out screaming and crying, begging for help. Her baby was critically ill. Was there a minister who would baptize it? Scamahorn performed the baptism on the spot. The grateful mother gave him two dollars and a warm peach pie. The party left her there with her dying child and plodded on toward Gordon.

As they headed west, the immigrants dispersed toward homesteads between Valentine and Gordon. Margaret and Gideon settled on Sheridan County's Pole Creek, on the tablelands south of the Niobrara River. They were joined there by Joe Fairhead and his three brothers, who walked the ninety miles from Valentine to Pole Creek, then turned around and walked back to Valentine to file on their homesteads. Other neighbors included the Lemons, from Indiana, the Vollintines (after whom the town of Valentine had been named), originally from Texas, and Josiah and Dr. Mary Elizabeth Baker, from Iowa.

Dr. Baker served as Pole Creek's physician, minister, and community social director. When a ten-year-old boy shot himself in the arm with a shotgun, Dr. Baker cut off part of the gangrenous limb with a meat saw, saving the boy's life. One morning in February she baptized Margaret and Gideon in the icy waters of the Niobrara. In her memoirs, published in "Recollections" of Sheridan County, Nebraska, Margaret remembered the baptism as a frigid but festive occasion: "It was very cold and the ice was about three feet thick. A hole was made in the ice and then a chair placed on the bottom of the river on which we stepped from the ice and down into the river. After we had been immersed, blankets were thrown around us and we drove three miles in a big wagon to Ed

Lemon's little log cabin and changed our clothes. We then started for the Waggoner sod house or dugout. As we drew near we found that Lo and Behold! all the neighbors had gathered around and brought baskets of grub with them."

During their first few years on their 160-acre homestead, Margaret and Gideon harvested good crops of corn and vegetables. They raised a few chickens, but the coyotes got most of them. With great effort they dug a shallow well, which caved in after a couple of years. Margaret gave birth to four children; two died in infancy.

After three years the Waggoners moved from their dugout into a more "respectable" sod house with three rooms, wood floors, and a shingle roof. They weren't getting rich, but they were getting by. Margaret's stepdaughter described the general living conditions of the time seventy years later: "The countryside was rich with wild ducks, prairie chickens, geese and antelope, deer, buffalo, and elk. Wild fruit grew in abundance. . . . There were many prairie fires started by lightning which took every member of their families to help, some using old wet sacks and some plowing wide strips of land to stop the fires. . . . And blizzards, some very bad storms, lasting for weeks."

As time passed, the game diminished and the ground became less fertile. In 1893 a severe drought struck just as the nation sank into a depression. Crops withered throughout western Nebraska as banks closed and prices for agricultural goods plummeted. The rains failed in 1894 and again in 1895.

So devastating were the crop failures that the *New York World* dispatched its ace reporter, Nellie Bly, to report on the drought. She wrote from Valentine of a desiccated landscape, "covered with the yellow stubble of corn-stalks that never matured and grain that never came to head. . . . Fortunate were they who had friends to help them out of this God-forsaken country. For I see no help for those remaining."

Bly interviewed one couple who had lost most of their crops to drought or hailstorms in nine of the previous eleven years. A neighbor lamented, "It does seem as if Nebraska is going to dry up completely." At a nearby sod house, Bly found six children in rags and their mother gravely ill with pneumonia: "The look on the woman's face, the pallor, and the strange, glassy glitter in her eyes, gave me a cold chill."

According to historian Marshall Bowen, there were more than five hundred farm and ranch foreclosures in Sheridan County between 1893 and 1899. Nine Sheridan County residents were charged with murder and forty-one were committed to mental institutions during this same period. By 1899 nearly two-thirds of homesteaders had abandoned the tablelands north and south of the Niobrara.

At Pole Creek, the Waggoners hung on while most of their neighbors drifted away. Margaret collected wild foods. Gideon hunted what little game he could find. They traded livestock and possessions for grain and sugar. Finally, in 1899, after what Margaret described as "fifteen years of toil and struggle," they gave up. They sold the homestead, paid off their debts, and went to work putting up hay for local ranchers.

Margaret worked as a ranch cook, and Gideon became postmaster of the town of Wood Lake. Slowly they began to recoup their losses from the drought years. By 1913 they had acquired a small ranch with a few cattle, and Margaret had opened a millinery store. When Gideon died in an automobile accident that year, the children were old enough to carry on the family's growing business.

In 1920 Margaret married former Pole Creek neighbor Joe Fairhead, and she and her youngest daughter moved to Gordon, where her new husband owned a meat market. Her daughter was killed in 1925 when her horse crashed into a telephone pole. Joe Fairhead died of heart disease in 1933. Margaret, now living alone, continued to run a grocery store and meat market. When she died in 1944 at age seventy-nine, she had become one of Gordon's most prominent and respected citizens.

Margaret Waggoner Fairhead was one of the select few in Sheridan County who survived the agricultural disasters of the 1890s. She did it through persistence and the perspicacity to make the transition to ranching when farming failed. She paid a heavy price: fifteen years of fruitless toil on the homestead, three children and two husbands lost.

In the sandy soil south of the Niobrara River, along the northern edge of the Sandhills, the grass came back quickly.

Within a few years after Margaret and Gideon had abandoned their homestead, cattle grazed where wheat and corn had burned in the summer heat. On the shortgrass and mixed-grass prairies north of the river, it took decades for the land to recover.

During the 1960s and 1970s, farmers again tried to plow the porous soil on the periphery of the Sandhills. In spite of center-pivot irrigation, many of these efforts also failed, and the land reverted to grass. Today there is probably less Sandhills soil under cultivation than was being farmed when Margaret and Gideon Waggoner sold out in 1899.

Up along Pole Creek nothing remains of the hopeful community that blossomed during the late 1880s and early 1890s. A modern two-story farmhouse overlooks a shallow ravine where cattle crowd into the shade of a few scrub willows. Fields of prairie sandreed and smooth brome toss and sway in the autumn breeze.

The history of the place cries out for something more, at the very least a plaque or a small monument to honor the gritty settlers who struggled through years of drought and disappointment. For now the rippling grasses and limitless horizon will have to do.

PINE LAKE

THE FIRST time I visited Pine Lake, I stopped for five minutes before heading on down the highway. There wasn't much to see, I thought, looking out over a shallow, half-mile-wide body of water flanked by a few cottonwoods, a ragged grove of ponderosa pines and junipers, and a dozen rickety picnic tables with peeling red paint.

The second time I stopped long enough to watch an osprey spearing catfish in a quiet inlet and to photograph a pair of dueling bull snakes rolling and slithering through the golden switchgrass. One of them took offense and came after me, cobra-style. Later I dived into the cold water and paddled around on my back as a flock of white-faced ibis sailed overhead. I was beginning to like the place.

The third time I stayed overnight. A pair of great horned owls perched on the ponderosa above the tent and hooted me to sleep. I awoke to the yipping of coyotes, the clucking of coots, gadwalls, and shovelers, and the reassuring moos of a few dozen Herefords. I was hooked.

Now I go back to Pine Lake whenever I'm in the Sandhills. Some travelers quickly grow tired of familiar vistas, but I'd rather get to know one place well than see a thousand places superficially. At Pine Lake I'm like a fisherman putting out to sea in the same weathered craft time and again. The immediate surroundings are stark and familiar, but there's always something new on the horizon.

The lake floats through a three-dimensional sea of whirling constellations, wind-driven clouds, and changing seasons. March brings snow geese, sandhill cranes, and sudden snowstorms. June offers dewy sunrises, cottonwood leaves rustling in the afternoon breeze, churring cicadas, and moss-encrusted snapping turtles laying their eggs in the sandy road bank. On cold October mornings frozen spiderwebs festoon the cattails like strands of pearls, and ice-encrusted dragonflies dangle from crystalline sunflowers. When the north wind blows in February, the words desolation and survival take on a richer meaning.

The lake is in constant motion in the most literal sense. It circles the earth's axis at a brisk 800 miles an hour, passing through calm and storm, sunrises and sunsets, moonrises and moonsets; and it zooms around the sun at 65,000 miles per hour, navigating through the seasons, the equinoxes and solstices, bird migrations, the coming and going of ice and snow. Slower but equally dramatic is the lake's journey through the stages of ecological succession. It will someday become a marsh, then a wet meadow sprinkled with cottonwoods, and finally tallgrass prairie. I can see signs of this evolution along the shoreline where the cattail marsh is filling in with silt and prairie grasses are poking through the muck. Meanwhile, Pine Lake is journeying through geologic time, catapulting around the core of the Milky Way galaxy and hurtling outward toward the edge of the universe.

If I were truly aware of all this motion, I would die of dizziness. But being human, I'm pretty much oblivious to my larger surroundings and must take pleasure in little things.

One April morning while walking through the woods, I flush a mallard off her nest. Her eight pale green eggs nestle against the roots of a ponderosa pine. I almost step on a second nest a few yards away. Before long the woods are frantic with fast-flying, hysterically quacking mallards, and I soon find five more nests tucked among the pines, far from water.

In autumn, as I explore the cattail marsh at the north end of the lake, I discover a secret passage created by white-tailed deer. The two-foot-wide tunnel snakes through the head-high cattails, intersecting several other trails to form a maze. A deer could spend days in here without being seen. As I crunch along, I hear a pickup truck pull to a stop on the edge of the marsh. "Thunk . . . thunk." The men get out. "Click . . . click." Hunting season! I crouch down, hold my breath, and tremble like a white-tailed deer.

In early May I wake to a gentle trilling outside my tent. I stick my head out, and there stands a female wild turkey gobbling food scraps scattered under the picnic tables. I hurry off to tell my friend Roger, who's camped in the woods a hundred yards away.

"Roger, there's a wild turkey down by the picnic table. You have to get up."

"No, I don't," he says, grinning up at me. "Look behind you." She's lurking at my feet. We name her Roxanne.

Over that weekend Roger, Roxanne, and I make up a tight threesome as we walk together through the woods and around the lake. We humans take the lead, with the turkey following at a discreet distance or trotting up to us, ostrich-like, whenever we stop. Roxanne develops a particular fondness for Roger. I occasionally find her rubbing against his leg while he strokes her neck feathers and the two of them converse in subdued, gallinaceous tones.

While out walking alone one afternoon, I find a cousin of Roxanne's nestled down in the switchgrass south of the campground, about two feet off a faint game trail. As I approach, the turkey extends her neck and hisses. A clutch of large spotted eggs protrudes from under her dusky feathers. It's the only wild turkey nest I've ever seen at the lake.

As Roger and I are packing to leave, we notice that Roxanne has camped in the back of my Subaru wagon. We're tempted to take her along, knowing all too well the probable fate of a fully socialized wild turkey in a state wildlife (hunting and fishing) area. But we're not sure the folks down at the state Game and Parks Commission will see things our way. We leave her standing by the garbage cans, casually pecking at a piece of stale French bread.

ROXANNE IS one of ninety bird species that nest at Pine Lake. Near the top of the list, and at the top of the food chain, are five owls. The great horned owls lay their eggs in abandoned crow and red-tailed hawk nests in the ponderosas above the campground. The scattered remains of crows, flickers, mice, voles, squirrels, and muskrats below the nests testify eloquently to the horned owls' position in the feeding hierarchy. When they hoot, everybody listens.

Across the lake a pair of eastern screech-owls peer out from their nest cavity in a dead cottonwood. At the south end of the lake, short-eared owls course over the cattails at dawn and dusk hunting voles and mice. They nest on the ground in a depression lined with a few feathers and blades of grass. Burrowing owls sometimes perch on fence posts or poke their heads up out of rodent burrows in the grazed pastures. One night the barks and screams of a long-eared owl wake me. The next morning I find her sitting alertly on an old crow's nest, a few yards from my tent and perilously close to the horned owls, which eat long-eared owl chicks.

The songbirds include robins, grackles, and other habitat generalists, which are as comfortable around the campground as in the woods, and the more elusive habitat specialists such as marsh wrens and swamp sparrows, which frequent the wilder niches around the lake. The vulnerability of these specialists adds to their appeal; some cling to the web of life by a single thread, a specific plant or ecosystem that is essential to their survival.

Along the shoreline, marsh wren males weave intricate, spherical nests from cattail leaves, cattail fluff, and grass. They enter and exit through quarter-sized holes on the side. They attach the nests to two or more cattail stalks a few feet above the water. A single male may construct ten or more nests to confuse predators. He does this while frenetically chattering away, often with his beak stuffed full of cattail fluff, and scurrying up and down the cattail stalks like a wind-up toy. If the marsh dries up, the raccoons or foxes get the eggs or young. If the cattails die off, the marsh wrens vanish.

Yellow warblers flit through the cottonwoods, where they construct exquisite, cup-shaped nests from shredded bark, grass, milkweed seeds, and spiderwebs. When a cowbird dumps its egg in the nest, the warblers sometimes build a second nest on top of the first one.

The yellow warblers arrive from Mexico and Central America just as the cottonwoods and willows leaf out and insects begin to swarm. Their high, breathless song, a rapid "sweet-sweet-sweet, I'm so very sweet," resonates with the wind rush in the cottonwood leaves, the raspy cicada sound, and the marsh wrens' metallic, staccato chattering. Should the cottonwoods disappear, so would the warblers. Without the warblers, the cottonwoods would lose their familiar sound and spirit.

White-breasted nuthatches lay their eggs on a soft bed of bark, hair, and feathers in a deserted woodpecker hole. One day the Game and Parks people came through and cut down all the dead trees in the campground. Now I miss the nuthatches' comical, nasal calls and their acrobatics as they skitter upside down along the branches gleaning insects and stashing seeds.

Then there are the long-billed curlews, swooping over the dunes like fluttering kites, piercing the calm with their whistling cries. Once heard, their high, drawn-out "cur-leeuuu," cousin to the wind in the grass and to waves crashing against distant shores, becomes part of the subliminal music that surfaces whenever the mind lets go of conscious thought. I hear their calls daily around the lake, and almost as often when I'm sitting quietly at home dreaming of invigorating days spent wandering in the hills.

The loquacious, two-foot-tall curlews are hard to miss as they perch on the dune tops or sail on the wind. But they're finicky about habitat and won't nest in just any old prairie. They like a mixture of grass types, short for foraging and longer for nesting; lakes or mudflats where they can probe for invertebrates with their nine-inch downcurved bills; and most of all, solitude. Unlike the cosmopolitan killdeers, which will lay their eggs in parking lots or construction sites, long-billed curlews don't take readily to what some call civilization. Nineteenth-century naturalists wrote that migrating flocks of these magnificent shorebirds once "blackened the sun" over New England and the Midwest. Now migrants are rarely seen east of the Mississippi, and remaining nesting populations cling to patches of grassland in the West. A closely related species, the once abundant Eskimo curlew, may already be extinct.

Since they nest out in the open, usually in a shallow scrape concealed by tufts of grass, long-billed curlews rely on bluff and bravado to deter predators. This boldness, combined with their vulnerability, draws me toward them. I spend quiet summer evenings at Pine Lake sitting on a hilltop, observing the resident pair's domestic activities and anticipating the spectacular strafing runs they make whenever a coyote, hawk, or other intruder ventures by.

A plant list for Pine Lake would easily exceed three hundred species. My favorite is the plains evening star, a weedy, moth-pollinated perennial that opens its translucent white flowers just before sunset. Along roadsides and on sparsely vegetated dunes, fields of the star-shaped blossoms glow in the twilight.

Another moth-pollinated plant, the yucca, or soapweed, grows on similar sites, where its fibrous taproot clings tenaciously to the sandy soil. In Plains Indian fashion, I use the taproot for soap and munch on the flower petals, which taste like asparagus.

On evening walks, I like to open the bell-shaped yucca flowers and look for pronuba moths. This little white moth is one of the most indispensable creatures on earth. It is the only insect that can pollinate the yucca's hard-to-reach ovaries. The female moth flies from flower to flower, gathering pollen and storing it in a clump behind her head. After inserting an egg in the ovary of a flower, she grabs a wad of pollen and stuffs it down into the flower's reproductive parts.

By pollinating the yucca flower, the moth ensures that her offspring will have fruit and seeds to eat, and she guarantees that the fertile yucca will propagate, creating more host plants. Fortunately, the pronuba moth does this without a lot of reflection. If the moth turned creative and started searching for other host plants, the yucca would soon become extinct. Without the hearty soapweeds to stabilize the soil on the most exposed dunes, the sand would shift and the grass would become sparser, changing the character of the entire ecosystem.

On moister sites, lavender three-petaled spiderwort blossoms unfurl in early summer, attracting bees, butterflies, mice, and love-struck humans. Young Dakota men used the spiderwort flower as a love charm, singing songs to it or rubbing its petals between their palms to win the heart of a favored young woman. According to ethnobotanist Melvin Gilmore, "the beauties of the flower and the girl [were] mutually transmuted . . . into one image in the suitor's mind." I've nibbled on these sweet, achingly beautiful flowers—once. Picking the blossoms felt wantonly destructive, like taking a razor blade to a Monet.

In addition to all the birds and wildflowers, the lake's environment supports more than twenty species of mammals. There are raccoons that rattle the trash cans every evening, deer mice that chew their way into my ice chest and nest in the bowels of the Subaru, an old badger that shuffles through the pines behind the campground, and the omnipresent coyotes.

A moderately observant human could spend a lifetime at the lake studying fungi alone. As for insects, the possibilities are limitless. Each ecosystem around the lake, from pine forest to grassland to cattail marsh, hosts its own unique assortment of ants, wasps, damselflies, dragonflies, butterflies, and grasshoppers. One summer morning I count a dozen species of dragonflies and damselflies perched on cattail leaves near the campground. The porous soil beneath the pines is a treasure trove of worms, mites, spiders, springtails, root aphids, and miniature beetles. I understand that an average square yard of prairie soil contains 9 million nematodes. So if I get bored at Pine Lake, it's my fault, not nature's.

But the howling autumn nights and rainy spring days can grow long and lonely. Part of it is feeling adrift out here without routine and familiar distraction. Part of it is missing my partner and my home, longing for a sense of unity with nature that seems unattainable. The serenity of this wild place opens the mind to the persistent sadness that living apart from nature engenders. I want to get closer to the grass, wind, and wildlife, but I know I can never get close enough.

I also grow paranoid and possessive about the lake's inhabitants. Each spring I approach Pine Lake with the same mix of excitement and apprehension that charges a reunion with a long-absent lover. I sidle up to the lake, wondering if I'll find the wood ducks nesting in the rotting trunk of the old cottonwood and the Cooper's hawk perched in the tallest ponderosa. I scour the dunes for the first shell-leaf penstemon and ceramic milk vetch, listen for the snort of a white-tailed deer and the trill of a wild turkey.

In short order one of my wild acquaintances ambles by or flies over, and I begin to breathe again.

PINE LAKE is one of thousands of Sandhills lakes and ponds. The number varies from year to year as differing amounts of precipitation and irrigation make groundwater levels rise and fall. Most lakes lie in the interdunal valleys where groundwater percolates in from the underlying aquifer. Many of these lakes were created during periods of drought when drifting dunes blocked creek drainages. These sand dams are porous, and the lakes gradually fill with sediment. Most are so shallow that to drown you'd have to stand on your head.

No one lake is quite like another. Lakes in the drier western region tend toward extreme alkalinity. Some support no shoreline vegetation at all, others only one or two species of sedge or rush. The most alkaline of these lakes contain millions of brine shrimp, savored by migrating shorebirds. Biologists once counted ten thousand avocets on 150-acre Border Lake, in Crescent Lake National Wildlife Refuge.

Lakes in the wetter eastern region support a much richer aquatic flora. Plains Indian foraging parties gathered wild rice, arrowhead root, and pond lilies from the soupy, algae-filled waters. Indians and white settlers also visited these lakes to trap mink and muskrat, hunt ducks and geese, capture giant snapping turtles, and net fish.

Sandhills lakes, ponds, and streams support an astonishing seventy-five species of fish, including many with whimsical names: alewife, coho salmon, grass pickerel, central stoneroller, emerald shiner, northern redbelly dace, bigmouth buffalo, shorthead redhorse, stonecat, plains killifish, pumpkinseed, orangethroat darter, and freshwater drum. New species are still being documented. In 1989 biologists exploring a small tributary of the North Loup River found live specimens of Topeka shiner, a small, pollution-intolerant fish thought to have been extirpated from Nebraska's waterways several decades ago.

Why so much variety? Just as the Sandhills sop up moisture, they also sop up species. Many of these fish are eastern and northern species that may have become isolated in the region at the end of the last ice age, when the Great Plains became more arid. Others are introduced game fish that have taken hold and thrived in the Sandhills' spring-fed streams and nutrient-rich lakes.

Pine Lake contains a representative assortment of the traditional game fish—bass, sunfish, and perch stocked by the Game and Parks Commission—along with a smattering of natives. These fish attract cormorants, white pelicans, common mergansers, ospreys, bald eagles, Forster's terns, black terns, and mink, as well as anglers who drive down from Hay Springs, Gordon, and Rushville.

On summer days a few of these human visitors come and go, leaving a stray pop can or two. But by early evening when the breezes soften, the last wayfaring pelicans cruise in and splash down, and white-tailed deer emerge from the shadows to browse in sunlit meadows, I usually have the place to myself.

During the colder seasons, it's the emptiness of Pine Lake, the wild, windswept desolation, that draws me. One night in April I drive in just before dawn. I step out of the car into a face-numbing wind and a rousing chorus of coyotes and curlews. White-capped waves slap the shoreline. The ponderosa pines creak and groan. As I peer up at their swaying branches, a meteor streams across the charcoal sky, scattering liquid cinders. Welcome back.

TALLGRASS DESERT

I was now in one of the blankest spots on the American map, a big section showing almost no rivers or roads or towns. This is the Nebraska Sandhill country, the original model for the map makers' Great American Desert. . . . There was so little to look at that when a crow flew past in front of me and dropped something from its beak I turned around and went back to see what it was: a fetal duckling, featherless, blue, with bulging sealed eyes, and tiny webbed feet.

—Ian Frazier, *The Great Plains*

I FIRST came to the Sandhills on a calm May evening when the grass shimmered in soft sunlight and the air smelled of sweet clover, sand verbena, pondweed, and cows. I thought I had discovered an earthly paradise.

This was hardly the view of James McKay, the first white explorer to visit the region. In 1795 McKay, a Scottish trapper, led an expedition up the Missouri River searching for beavers, mink, and otters. After spending the winter of 1796 in the villages of the Maha Indians, McKay's party followed the Niobrara River up into the northeastern Sandhills. McKay described the country south of present-day

Valentine as "a great desert of drifting sand without trees, soil, rocks, or animals of any kind, excepting some little varicolored turtles."

Other explorers expressed similar sentiments. Governeur Kemble Warren, a topographical engineer on a punitive expedition against the Sioux in 1856, disparaged the terrain south of the Niobrara River: "The sand is formed into limited basins, over the rims of which you are constantly passing up one side and down the other, the feet of the animals frequently sinking so as to make the progress excessively laborious. The scenery is exceedingly solitary, silent, and desolate, and depressing to one's spirits." Warren's disdain for the Sandhills region applied equally to the relatively fertile river valleys. Of the Middle Loup River he said, "Our greatest wish is to get away from it as soon as possible and never return."

In 1866 geologist Ferdinand V. Hayden chimed in. Hayden, a University of Pennsylvania professor known as the "businessman's geologist" for his advocacy of western settlement, followed the north bank of the Niobrara River on his journey to the White River Badlands. He characterized the Sandhills as "20,000 square miles . . . of loose moving sand, which is driven by the winds into round or conical hills." The vegetation, he said, was scarce except for "a few plants clinging with a sort of hopeless tenacity to the sides of the hills, and in some cases protecting them from the winds."

It's hard to believe these explorers were describing the same country that today appears as an oasis of green within an arid expanse of closely cropped prairies and parched wheatfields. Maybe they weren't. Tree-ring data from the Great Plains indicate that the region experienced three major droughts during the nineteenth century. The 1820s and 1860s droughts may have been even more severe than the 1930s Dust Bowl drought. In 1820 Edwin James wrote of "many tracts of naked sand" along the South Platte River. Hayden visited the Sandhills during the 1860s drought, possibly the worst one to hit the Great Plains during the past 250 years. Recent geological research confirms that the dunes have shifted several times during the past three centuries.

Caroline Sandoz Pifer, whose father, Jules Sandoz, settled in the Rushville area during the 1880s, says there was "much less grass" on the hillsides when her father first arrived. Photographs of their ranch taken shortly after the turn of the century show the ridge tops completely barren of vegetation.

Hay Springs area rancher D. L. Bliss wrote that the "Sandhills of the 1900's were not in the same league with the Sand Hills of today." He described the difficulty of herding cattle in parched, grasshopper-infested country: "By late afternoon your mouth felt like you had taken a big bite out of a bale of cotton and those awful rasping Sand Hill locusts would let go and make you feel even drier." Bliss credits ranchers with improving the quality of the range.

These images of a near desert being transformed by settlers into a productive grassland confound environmental stereotypes. We expect humans to degrade natural land-scapes rather than improve them. Some Sandhills ranchers believe grazing by cattle increased the grass cover, in the same way that mowing your lawn makes the grass grow thicker. Many ranchers believe that suppressing prairie fires let the prairie grasses spread upslope from the moist valleys. In Great Plains and Missouri Valley tallgrass prairies, periodic burning typically has a regenerative effect, leading to an overall increase in the volume of low vegetation. But in the Sandhills the relatively steep topography may have created very hot fires that scorched the tops of sparsely vegetated dunes, reducing vegetative cover.

Tom Bragg, a biologist at the University of Nebraska at Omaha, analyzed fire scars and tree rings to determine the historical frequency of prairie fires. He concluded that during the nineteenth century fires swept through a typical area of the northern Sandhills every three to five years. Fires probably burned more frequently during the nineteenth century than during previous centuries. In fact, fires deliberately set by Plains Indians during the almost continual wars of that period may have changed the natural fire regime enough to influence the character of prairie vegetation.

Overgrazing during the late nineteenth and early twentieth centuries may have contributed to the denuded appearance of some areas of the Sandhills. James Stubbendieck, of the University of Nebraska, says a combination of improved range management and fire suppression has resulted in "a nearly completed cover of prairie vegetation in the

Sandhills." The Sandhills, he says, "have developed into one of the best managed large tracts of rangeland in the world."

However, some scientists believe nineteenth-century descriptions of a Sandhills desert reflect differences in environmental perception rather than significant changes in the landscape. A handful of nineteenth-century explorers praised the beauty of the lush river valleys and grass-covered dunes, and some modern writers still refer to the region as a wasteland.

IN THE SANDHILLS I often wake at 4 A.M. needing to poke my head out of the tent to make sure the prairie is still there. For anyone seeking connection with nature, living in a culture that worships economic expansion and urban "development" can create a state of near constant anxiety.

For most of us nature has become something we drive a couple of hundred miles to look at. We tend to see the natural world two-dimensionally—as a scenic vista, a picture postcard, a peak conquered. Our protected lands, mostly parks and wilderness areas, are far removed from our homes.

This tradition of living separately from the natural environment evolved in part from the European American custom of viewing lands as either "productive" or "nonproductive." Nineteenth-century North American writers commonly used desert imagery to characterize any landscape that was not like the green fields of New England. Unoccupied, unplowed land, be it old-growth forest, marshland, tallgrass prairie, or sagebrush upland, qualified as "desert."

The same rules applied to the Sandhills. Until someone could find an economic use for them, they remained a moonscape in the minds of those searching for agrarian potential rather than aesthetic beauty. What saved the Sandhills was not a conservation ethic but a random convergence of economics and geology. In short, you can't plow sand, and cattle ranchers must conserve the prairie to survive.

Cattle had been pastured in the Sandhills since the early 1870s, but local legend says that the region's economic potential suddenly became clear during the spring of 1879, when a series of blizzards drove cattle from neighboring ranches into the hills.

James C. Dahlman was working at the Newman Ranch near Gordon. The ranch had stationed line riders on the edge of the area cowboys referred to as the "sand hills desert," to keep cattle from drifting into the region during storms. In March 1879 a fierce blizzard blew in, forcing the line riders indoors and pushing several thousand head of cattle into the Sandhills.

Dahlman and his crew headed into the hills on April 15. On the second day out, they got lost in a howling blizzard. They holed up for three days, doing all they could to keep from freezing. When the storm cleared, they began to encounter herds of cattle, "perfectly contented," wrote Dahlman, "in their new home amidst the splendid grass and water in the valleys." From that time on, "instead of trying to keep cattle out of the sandhills in winter time, they were thrown in."

Cattle and Sandhills went together, as D. L. Bliss put it, "like beef and biscuits." Once Sandhills cattle ranches had become established, people began to rave about the beauty and productiveness of the land.

The largest of these ranches, the Spade, covered two thousand square miles, extending all the way north to the White River in South Dakota. The Spade's owners maintained their empire through intimidation and extralegal appropriation of rangeland, actions that infuriated homesteaders and the owners of smaller ranches.

The Spade's founder and principal owner, Bartlett Richards, came west in 1880 at age seventeen. Raised in a prosperous New England family, Richards planned to spend a year traveling, working, and nursing his fragile health before enrolling in Williams College. He found life on the open range to his liking, and his health problems— chronic intestinal inflammation and "sore eyes"—abated.

He started out as a cowhand for one of the large Wyoming outfits, quickly won a promotion to ranch foreman, and within one year had begun investing his family's and friends' savings in his own herds. By his twentieth birthday, Richards was running a half-million-dollar cattle company for a group of British investors, supervising six thousand head grazing the open ranges of eastern Wyoming and South Dakota.

Richards's intelligence, family connections, and work ethic (in one of his early letters home he spoke of having planted 117 fence posts in a single day) no doubt contributed to his meteoric rise in the cattle industry. His timing couldn't have been better. The industry was new, the range was still open, and beef prices were high.

By 1888 Richards had acquired several cattle ranches in northwestern Nebraska and had been appointed president of a bank in Chadron. But the open range was rapidly being fenced off by homesteaders flooding into western Nebraska and eastern Wyoming. Richards consolidated his holdings into one enormous ranch in the Sandhills southeast of Chadron.

He and his partners found they could control hundreds of square miles of rangeland by filing on only those quarter sections that contained water. The Spade solicited ranch employees, widows, and Civil War veterans to "homestead" these parcels. Since the remaining arid uplands were unsuitable for homesteading, the Spade could run its cattle unfettered from water hole to water hole without having to buy the intervening land. Later the Spade's owners fenced in this publicly owned land to control the movement of their stock.

Cattle were driven from as far south as Texas and Mexico to fatten up on Sandhills grasses and then shipped east on railroad lines that had recently penetrated the region. Profits were impressive. During the 1890s and early 1900s, Spade Ranch stockholders received annual dividends of 25 percent or more.

However, ranch life was tough and often violent. Cowboys worked eighteen-hour days riding through blizzards or birthing calves in subzero temperatures. In 1903 a poker game turned deadly when a seasonal worker hit another cowhand over the head with a two-by-four. Another worker was killed by lightning in 1904, and a third strangled when his coat got caught in the bevel wheel of a windmill tower. Prairie fires, wildly fluctuating beef prices, cattle rustlers, and nearly constant conflict with homesteaders made ranching a risky business.

In 1904 Congress passed the Kincaid Act, allowing western Nebraska homesteaders to claim not 160 but 640 acres. The intent was to open up the last remaining large area of prairie in the central plains to homesteaders. As settlers flocked into the Sandhills, the latent enmity between ranchers and farmers escalated. Settlers, who now began to file on the arid uplands, accused the cattle barons of illegally fencing these public lands and filing fraudulent claims on them.

Some disputes turned bloody. Along Pine Creek Emile Sandoz, brother of the notorious homesteader and Spade Ranch antagonist "Old Jules" Sandoz, was shot in the back by Ralph Nieman, an employee of the Schwartz Ranch. Some characterized Nieman as a "hired gun" for the local cattle barons. Others maintained he was merely a hothead

settling a personal feud. The jury convicted him on a reduced charge of manslaughter, on the questionable grounds
that the victim had lingered for three days before he died.

In Mullen, a few miles east of the Spade Ranch, a
homestead locator and surveyor named O. F. Hamilton disappeared in mysterious circumstances. His body was later
found in a shallow grave, identified by a dozen local residents, and buried in the Mullen cemetery. A saloon owner
and his cowboy friends were accused of the murder. As the
trial began, the defense attorneys requested that the body be
dug up for reidentification. The exhumed body looked like
Hamilton's, but it was now attached to the head of an
African American man. The case was dismissed. Years later
a witness revealed that the saloon owner, who feared Hamilton would testify against him at an upcoming licensing
hearing, had indeed orchestrated the murder and switching
of heads. His friends, who detested Hamilton, were all too
happy to go along with the charade.

In response to the escalating violence and to pressure
from western constituents, the federal government began
enforcing an 1885 law prohibiting fencing of public lands.
In 1905 Richards, several of his associates, and several neighboring ranchers were convicted of illegally fencing hundreds
of square miles. Richards pleaded guilty, promised to take
the fences down, and paid a fine of $300. A year later he
and his partners were convicted of fraudulent land acquisition. After four years of appeal, Richards and two partners
were sent to a jail in Hastings, Nebraska, to serve a one-year
sentence.

At their original trial their attorney, Judge Albert W. Crites of Chadron, argued that the government was prosecuting the cattle ranchers for making the best possible use of land that was unsuitable for homesteading: "I doubt if one-fifth of the men who filed on these lands will ever prove up on them. It is a country of sand hills and it is a physical impossibility to make a home or residence on them."

But public opinion, urged on by the press, railed against Richards and his "cattle baron" associates. The November 29, 1910, edition of the *Hastings Daily Tribune* reported inaccurately that the local jail had been converted into a country club, with Persian rugs, a private telephone, and a Japanese chef to accommodate the "millionaire prisoners."

Richards's letters from jail to his family, reprinted in *Bartlett Richards, Nebraska Sandhills Cattleman*, paint the picture of a practical man who was as much embarrassed as angered by his predicament. In his letters Richards never spoke directly of his humiliation and never admitted guilt. In fact his three children, then living in Coronado, California, didn't even know their father was in prison. They thought he was away on an extended business trip.

Richards wrote to them of family projects, including model airplane building, a new telescope, and plans to buy a new car. He sent them an article on bird migration, urging them to "get your mother to read this to you . . . for I want you to remember the interesting habits of birds."

The closest Richards came to writing about his legal problems was an oblique statement about sin and guilt in an earlier letter to his mother: "We'll all get there [heaven] some day—though some of us take one road—perhaps the back stairs—while others who are cocksure they have the only way, may find they don't get there any quicker. So we will be lenient with the beliefs of all and satisfy ourselves and consciences that we and all we love—and don't love— will get to the big round-up by ridge road—valley—or even up the canyon trail."

A month before his release from jail, Richards wrote to his wife about his plans. The letter concluded with these simple words:

> I am sending the children some postal cards John David sent me. Those "white magnolias" must be a picture of their imagination, don't you fancy?
>
> I had a poor night Sunday but feeling all right again—only aspirin.
>
> Love to the children. Your lover,
>
> Bartlett

A few days later he underwent surgery for a bowel obstruction and died of heart failure. He was forty-nine.

Declining beef prices, enforcement of federal fencing laws, and the absence of strong management led to dissolution of the Spade Ranch during the 1920s. A former employee, Lawrence Bixby, purchased what he could afford, piece by piece, until he owned 25,000 acres of the original ranch.

After the Spade and other megaranches broke up, families moved into the hills to work landholdings of a few thousand acres apiece. Today family operations continue to thrive, but declining profits have led to a consolidation of holdings and sale of family lands to corporate investors. Some properties now encompass one hundred square miles or more, and residents fear the revival of large corporate livestock operations.

If you look at a modern map of Sheridan County you will see the Spade Ranch clearly marked a few miles north of Ellsworth. The town is pretty much as Bartlett Richards left it in 1910. There is the Spade Ranch store with its attached five-seat café, a small wooden post office, a weathered barn with a giant plastic horse head protruding above the entrance, an old windmill, a few wood-frame houses, and a set of railway tracks paralleling the main highway.

If you take a side road and venture off into the Spade Ranch domain, you will see Angus and Hereford cattle grazing amid stacks of hay, herons soaring over subirrigated meadows, and a monotony of uninhabited hills—the land that so many dismissed as desert and that Bartlett Richards recognized as "the finest cattle country in the world."

WHITETAILS

A young man was walking through the woods when he came upon a beautiful young maiden. He walked toward her, and she headed off into the forest. As he followed, she transformed herself into a sleek white-tailed deer. He ran after her, but she stayed just ahead of him, just out of reach, leading him deeper and deeper into the forest. He ran faster and faster, but he could never catch up. The young brave became hopelessly lost, running around in circles, until he went crazy in there, chasing that white-tailed deer.

—from a Cheyenne story

LOONEY TUNES music blares from the radio as I cruise down the Platte River Valley in the March predawn, racing toward a rendezvous with five thousand sandhill cranes at the Lewellen bridge. It's the *Waxworks Show* out of Emporia, Kansas, featuring big band sounds of the 1930s and 1940s. With the inevitable selection "In the Mood" blasting away, I put my foot down, hoping to reach the bridge in time to photograph the cranes' sunrise flight from their island roosts.

A white-tailed deer dances in the headlights like an apparition. I can't believe this is happening. The sickening thump, the tinkle of shattered glass, the car screeching to a halt on the shoulder.

I jump out. There is no sign of him, not even a trace of blood. I run up and down the roadside, peering through the mist. The deer has vanished as quickly as he appeared. It can't have been my imagination. The right headlight is smashed, and there's an ugly dent in the hood.

Finally I see him, a robust buck bounding through the pools of dense fog at the river's edge. He clears a barbed-wire fence, jumps an irrigation ditch, and dissolves into the shadows.

At the Lewellen bridge the Platte flows bloodred in dawn's first light. Massive chunks of ice float down, heaving and rumbling as they rub against the steel pylons. Ribbons of cranes stream across the crimson sky. A lone bald eagle glides upriver through the rising mist.

When the sun has cleared the horizon, I climb into the car and head back to town. A barn swallow swoops low over the road and thumps against the hood. I can see it in the rearview mirror, writhing on the pavement.

Back at the motel in Oshkosh, I review the morning's accomplishments: a whitetail buck maimed, a barn swallow killed, an ethereal sunrise poorly appreciated. It seems wise to get out of town before I do any more damage.

As I drive north, now creeping along at twenty-five miles an hour, the road becomes an obstacle course of dashing kangaroo rats, scurrying deer mice, and bewildered horned larks. I dodge and swerve, somehow making it to Pine Lake without killing any more birds or mammals.

The fog has settled over the lake's frozen surface, obscuring the ponderosas and junipers on the far shore. A few dozen silhouetted ducks paddle around in a small opening in the ice. A flock of crows perch in the bare cottonwoods.

Eager to reach the campground, I speed down the narrow dirt road circling the lake. A white-tailed doe bursts from the tall grass to my right. She floats over the hood as the car skids to a stop. The deer bounds into the marsh and pauses to give me a long questioning look before prancing off into the cattails.

OF COURSE I'm hardly the first person who ever mowed down a deer on U.S. 26. The clerk at the Oshkosh Superette says he bagged two during the past week. To prove it he shows me the dents in the hood of his Cadillac.

With white-tailed deer proliferating and no wolves and few mountain lions left to cull the herd, hunters and automobiles are their sole remaining predators. Every year cars kill several thousand deer in Nebraska. Still, whitetails are prospering, and people everywhere talk about the deer overpopulation problem.

During the late nineteenth century, hunting by European American settlers nearly eliminated whitetails from much of their historic range. The United States population of whitetails plummeted from an estimated 40 million in 1800 to about 500,000 in 1900; the Nebraska population dwindled to about 50 deer in 1900. Since then, habitat conservation and controls on hunting have contributed to a spectacular recovery. Now there are about 20 million whitetails in the United States and about 250,000 in Nebraska. They inhabit every state except Hawaii, Nevada, and Utah. Throughout the whitetails' range, biologists worry about a disappearing forest understory and an alarming spread to people of tick-borne diseases, including Lyme disease. Some midwestern cities have begun to allow limited hunting within city limits to control whitetail populations.

White-tailed deer, which were native to eastern deciduous forests and Missouri Valley river bottoms, invaded the western plains after European Americans began suppressing prairie fires, eliminating bison herds, and regulating stream flows through dams and water diversions. These actions permitted trees and shrubs to flourish along prairie streams where formerly, bison, fire, and scouring floods had stripped away vegetation. The deer moved west along these newly lush riparian corridors.

In 1846 Francis Parkman described the South Platte River Valley near the Nebraska–Wyoming border as "a narrow, sandy plain" with scattered vegetation. Today the river corridor is lined with cottonwoods and willows. Whitetails browse in the shrubby understory while blue jays and fox squirrels scream and chatter overhead. Elements of the eastern deciduous forest have been relocated a couple of hundred miles west onto the High Plains.

Much the same thing has happened in the Sandhills. Once home to large grass-eating herbivores such as bison and elk, along with grizzly bears, wolves, and mountain lions, the region has been stripped of its megafauna and invaded by eastern elements, including European Americans, cows, and white-tailed deer.

When describing their lonely life in the Sandhills, homesteaders used to say it was "ten miles to the nearest neighbor and a hundred miles to the nearest tree." The planting of trees around farmhouses and lakes and in human-created national forests has contributed to dramatic changes in wildlife populations. Forest-adapted predators such as red foxes, raccoons, and red-tailed hawks have displaced some grassland specialists. Their predatory activities have a ripple effect throughout the ecosystem, influencing populations of dozens of other species. When it comes to ecosystem disturbance, the white-tailed deer are just the tip of the iceberg.

Since whitetails occupy ecosystems that barely existed in the Sandhills before European settlement, their effects on native vegetation are difficult to measure. Their impact on shrub vegetation has been masked by the grazing of cows, which have cut a considerable swath through Sandhills ravines and canyons where wild plums, chokecherries, and other native shrubs once thrived.

The whitetails seem most at home in the river valleys, where trees provide cover and irrigated crops offer a munchable feast. Purdum rancher Bob Cox says he can expect to lose the first eight to ten rows of corn to whitetails each summer. Most everyone complains about whitetails in the gardens. An eighty-five-year-old woman who lives south of Merriman told me she got so tired of chasing one buck out of her tomato patch that she finally poked a rifle out the window and blew him away. "An excusable crime," she said, "under the circumstances."

BEHIND THE Pine Lake campground lies the inner kingdom, the white-tailed deer's sanctum sanctorum. A thicket of junipers and ponderosas provides cover for these reclusive forest dwellers. Hoofprints form zigzag trails in the sand. Every once in a while, when least expected, a graceful head pokes out from the vegetation, or a blue jay screams and a flared white rump disappears over the nearest hill. Were my senses not muted by years of suburban living, I could smell the scent marks on the juniper branches, the sweetness of deer sweat and urine, the musk of the buck who came visiting in the moonlight.

Whereas the local mule deer often aggregate in herds of five to thirty as they browse the grassy uplands, the Pine Lake whitetails mostly keep to themselves. During spring and summer a single doe and her young claim the inner kingdom. The local buck patrols a larger, overlapping territory, but the doe seems to tolerate his presence only during the fall mating season and early winter. The rest of the year she will repel him and other interlopers, sometimes lashing out with her sharp hooves.

When I can find the doe, I like to follow her at a discreet distance, observing her taste in food. The brain of a whitetail contains more local botanical knowledge than that of the average biology undergraduate. To survive, these deer must seek out the most palatable and nutrient-rich browse. In spring the Pine Lake deer nibble on sumac, willow stems, wild roses, dandelions, and succulent grasses. In summer they wade into the shallows to munch on arrowhead and pond lilies, and they scour the forest floor for mushrooms and fallen fruits. Shrub stems, bark, roots, and evergreen leaves get them through the winter, but just barely. A typical whitetail loses 12 to 20 percent of its body weight between November and April.

The graceful form of a white-tailed deer reflects its food preferences. Unlike the lumbering bison and robust elk, which require enormous digestive systems to process coarse prairie grasses, whitetails are built for feeding on the more delicate shrubs and wildflowers of the woodlands and marshes. Narrow jaws enable them to nibble selectively. Their slimmed-down digestive system fits into a streamlined body adapted for quick escape from predators waiting in ambush.

When I accidentally get too close, the Pine Lake white-tails sprint off with a conspicuous clatter of hooves, a flare of the rump and tail, and an exaggerated, bounding gait. Studies suggest these behaviors are deliberate. In *The Natural History of Deer*, British ecologist Rory Putnam says conspicuous flight warns other deer in the vicinity and sends two messages to the predator: "I've seen you; you've lost the element of surprise" and "Look how fit I am; I'm fast and healthy and not worth pursuing."

The deer seem spookily aware of my activities, and it's often when I'm doing something stupid, like chasing my tent over the hills or fishing my camera out of a swamp, that I look up and see the doe or a yearling staring at me with that perplexed, slightly critical look.

The idea that deer watch humans with an understanding eye was widely accepted among Native American cultures. In *Lame Deer, Seeker of Visions*, Lakota shaman John Lame Deer writes: "If you are planning to kill an eagle, the minute you think of that he knows it, knows what you are planning. The deer has this wisdom, too . . . if you shoot him, you won't hit him. He just stands right there and the bullet comes right back and hits you. It is like somebody saying bad things about you and they come back at him."

Lame Deer says killing a bison or a deer is like killing a relative who willingly gives up life so that others may survive. Hunters always recited a prayer of thanks after making a kill. "We apologized to his spirit, tried to make him understand why we did it, honoring with a prayer the bones of those who gave their flesh to keep us alive."

Many Native American myths tell of people changing into deer and deer into people. In a Ponca story, a lovely deer woman appears at tribal dances, where she seduces unsuspecting men, leads them off into the woods, and stomps them to death with her razor-edged hooves. A Pawnee story tells of a deer maiden who tricks a man into marrying her, lives with him as a human in his village, and then returns to the woods, leaving him desolate.

One story popular among many tribes tells how a herd of deer adopted a newborn child. The baby was born to a beautiful maiden who had been courted by the sun. The maiden, fearing no one would believe her explanation of the child's origins, decided to cast him aside. She wrapped the baby in cotton wool and laid the bundle beside a small stream.

A doe and two spotted fawns came by. Seeing the child, the doe decided to adopt him. She licked his tiny body and blew her warm breath on his face. Then she picked him up and carried him off to her home in the mountains.

Nurtured by the doe's rich milk, the sun child grew rapidly. Within a few days he was running around and playing with his foster brother and sister. He soon became leader of the entire herd, running out in front on his hard, hooflike feet, his long mane waving in the wind.

One day the maiden's uncle, while out hunting, spied the young man running with the deer herd. He returned to the village and told his people what he had seen. They decided to organize a hunt to begin in four days.

As always, the deer knew when and where they were to be hunted, and they knew the people would seek out their young leader. After much discussion and consultation with the spirits, the deer instructed the boy to stand in the middle of the herd until his relatives attacked. Then he was to run from the herd and submit peacefully. The hunters killed many brave deer, including the two fawns. But they allowed the boy's adoptive mother to escape. Finally they caught up to him. Frightened, he called out, "You have killed my brother and sister, what will you do with me?"

The hunters took the young man back to the village and reunited him with his mother. He married and became a great leader. It was said that he hunted with little effort, for he knew what rites and attentions would make the deer welcome death at the hands of a hunter.

ONE JUNE afternoon, while sitting among the ponderosas at Pine Lake reading a book, I hear what sounds like someone sneezing on the hillside behind me. The noise, barely audible over the wind rush in the pines, repeats every ten minutes or so. When I finally turn to look, the doe stands thirty feet away. I begin to talk to her.

"You're a beautiful white-tailed deer. Come closer; you know I wouldn't hurt you."

She takes a few tentative steps forward, her ears twitching and her tail swishing. I keep talking in reassuring tones. The doe edges closer until she stands almost within reach. I hush. She freezes in place, every muscle tensed. I try to read the emotion behind her impassive brown eyes and restless ears. Is it fear, curiosity, or a spark of connection between us?

A gust of wind ripples the tent canvas. She snorts, swivels, and gallops back over the hill.

The next morning I stumble on a tiny spotted fawn stretched out in the switchgrass fifty yards from camp. The fawn lies absolutely still, gazing up helplessly with its dewy, aquamarine eyes. I hold my breath and back away. The doe stands in the shadows, watching, as I pack up my tent and leave the woods.

A SENSE OF HOME

THE ONE-LANE gravel road to Mari Sandoz's grave passes through a forest of sunflowers. They brush against the windows
and tickle the undercarriage, making a crunching sound as
the car rattles along. The sunflowers crowd up the desiccated hillsides, adding a welcome splash of yellow to the
browns and russets of late summer.

The road creeps over a low rise and down into a bowl-
shaped valley with green grass, golden haystacks, and a
white farmhouse tucked in against the hills. Red letters
printed on a whitewashed board say "Mari's grave," and an
arrow points to the left. Indistinct tire tracks ramble

through a meadow and across a cattle guard overgrown with sweet clover and switchgrass.

Flora Sandoz, Mari's eighty-four-year-old sister, is opening a gate to move some steers from one pasture to another. She apologizes for the condition of the road and the cattle guard. "You should be able to make it through if you stay over to the left. Park up above the orchard."

A path leads through a squeaky wooden gate fastened by a length of rope tied to a rusting pulley. The path continues up the hillside to a small fenced plot containing a large headstone carved from black granite. The gravesite offers a sweeping view of the fruit orchard that Mari Sandoz's father, Jules, planted in 1910. Beyond lies the small, fertile pasture and the wild, empty hills where Mari drew inspiration for western classics like *Old Jules, Crazy Horse, Cheyenne Autumn,* and *Lovesong to the Plains.*

The valley below seems deserted and very still. I hear only the droning of a tractor off in the distance and the buzzing of bees down in the orchard. The inscription reads simply "Mari Sandoz, 1896–1966." No plastic flowers here. Just the prairie grasses, mowed back a little around the headstone, and a single sunflower waving in the breeze.

MARI SANDOZ learned to write while huddled in the attic of her Niobrara River home. Her father had forbidden her creative pursuits, saying he considered writers and artists "the maggots of society." Mari feared her father's violent temper. He once aimed a cocked rifle at her chest. He whipped her repeatedly and broke her finger with a chokecherry branch. But she wrote anyway. She had the gift, and there was so much to write about.

Jules Sandoz, a Swiss immigrant, came to the Niobrara River country, on the northern edge of the Sandhills, in 1884. He homesteaded on the flatlands south of Hay Springs and set himself up as a locator, helping other settlers find and procure homesteads. "Old Jules," as his neighbors called him, walked with a limp caused by falling into a well shortly after he arrived on the flats. He married and divorced three times before his thirtieth birthday. His constant battles with ranchers and with the corrupt judicial system earned him a reputation as a reckless and fearless pioneer trying to gain a foothold on the chaotic frontier.

An expert marksman, Jules liked to intimidate his enemies, the local cattle barons, by riding over to the neighboring Spade Ranch to practice target shooting within sight of the ranch house. A brilliant horticulturist, he planted the first fruit orchards in the Nebraska Panhandle and received numerous awards from regional and national horticultural organizations. He was a friend to local Cheyenne and Lakota leaders and a sometimes congenial host to visitors from Europe and the East Coast. His violent streak and bad temper were legendary. His fourth wife, Mary, and his six children often feared him. Neighbors, including the cattle barons, gave him a wide berth.

In 1910 Jules Sandoz gave up farming on the flats and moved his family to the 640-acre Kinkaid homestead in the Sandhills. An ad he placed in the *Rushville Standard* reflected some of his frustrations:

> We offer our ranch on Niobrara River for 10 dollars an acre, for 640 acres deeded land, a house and all fenced and cross fenced. . . . Six thousand fruit trees and shrubbery. . . .Terms cash. Possession given anytime. Reasons for selling: Can't get mail service nor school for our children and the County authorities have refused for years to protect our property, lives, and liberty.

Mari, the eldest, was fourteen at the time. Frail and withdrawn, she had turned to books as an escape from the dreary routine of chores, watching over the younger children, and staying clear of her father. When she began school at age nine she spoke only Swiss German. By the time she was eleven she was devouring everything she could find written in English, including Joseph Conrad, her father's government agricultural bulletins, and the socialist newspapers she sneaked into the house. She began to write stories, and one was published on the Junior Writer's Page of the *Omaha Daily News*.

During long hunting trips into the Sandhills, Jules told her stories about the range wars, the early hunts, the prairie fires, droughts, and blizzards. The stories continued around a wood-burning stove at night as Mari sat silently in the shadows, recording every detail in her mind: the distraught neighbor who killed herself and her three sons with gopher poison during the brutal winter of 1886, the ranch hand who shot her uncle Emile in the back, the Christmas blizzard of 1884, the Wounded Knee Massacre. Mari kept collecting the stories, kept writing them down. But she wouldn't tell her father about her writing until much later.

After a stint as a Sandhills schoolteacher and a five-year marriage to the son of a local rancher, Mari Sandoz, then twenty-three, moved to Lincoln to escape her father, further her education, and write. She wrote and nearly starved for fourteen years. During that time she completed sixty or so short stories—few of which ever appeared in print—an unpublished novel, and numerous nonfiction pieces about life in the pioneer West. Through all the disappointments and rejections, she never lost faith in her ability, though she often described her misfortunes with a bitter, self-deprecating wit. Of one of her novels she wrote, "I'm sure it will stay in print long after my death, if it has been published by then."

At the height of her frustration, she burned most of her manuscripts, then fired off a note to her agent in New York proclaiming that nothing of her work remained "except a few stories that I have given to a handful of loyal souls, such as everyone accumulates, no matter how unpromising their object of devotion may be."

These were grim times. For a few months Mari had gone back to full-time teaching to "have the security of meals again." She later related in her autobiography, "My teeth were going to pieces. I was down to 90 pounds, and the inertia turned out to be spots on my lungs and the doctor said I should go to a T.B. sanitarium."

In October 1928 Mari received news that her father lay near death in an Alliance Hospital. She headed back home to see him one last time.

> I knew my best material was my father, but he refused to let me write, except on the sly. . . .
>
> Then came the message that he was dying in the Alliance Hospital. I took the train and thought about his days since he drove west in 1884, across the spring Sandhills. Now it was fall and forty years later. I thought about him and his dreams, his visions, the stories he told. . . .
>
> At the hospital I saw an old, old man, his face a shell of pale wax, the beard a few short straggling beard hairs. He opened his eyes, recognizing no one, but remaining slits to see they did not leave him alone.
>
> I was shaken. This was the man who had roared and laughed and cursed like a thunder cloud through most of the years I had known him, building where settlers deserted, built where winter and hail decimated his orchards, now no more than a pale drift of cloud.
>
> A day passed, two, and the word that Old Jules was dying brought flowers from so many who had been given flowers from Old Jules' garden the last forty years. I occupied some of my time caring for them. Then as I came from the bathroom with my arms full of roses, I saw father was awake and conscious.
>
> "Oho, you are Mari—" he said, still with some of the old double r sound.
>
> Yes, yes, I was still in Lincoln.

He asked that I sit where he could see me when he awoke. Once he stirred, his eyes clear, I was to come home in the summer, see all the fine fruit. But then he asked me the most dreadful question, was I still writing?

I hesitated, remembering the long conflict this had been, from the confinement in the cellar, the grief he had put upon mother about it, his roaring temper. Weak as he was, he would die in it, and I would always have to know that I had killed my father.

But we never lied to him, evaded the truth, yes, but never lied outright.

So I said, "Yes I am still writing—" and as though this had never been contention between us he said, "Why don't you write my life sometime?"

Old Jules, based on the life of Mari's father, won the Atlantic Prize for nonfiction in 1935. It remains popular today, and many historians include it among the most accurate descriptions ever written of pioneering life on the Great Plains.

Mari Sandoz moved to Denver and then to New York. Though critics reacted favorably to her raw portrayal of life in the West, many Nebraskans took offense. Before she left Lincoln, she received threatening letters, and someone broke into her apartment and rifled her files.

Although she became something of an urbanite, Mari Sandoz never lost her love for the place she described in *Old Jules* as "a great sea caught and held forever in a spell." When she died in 1966, she was buried, as she had requested, on the sunny hillside overlooking the Sandoz home place south of the headwaters of the Snake River.

THE HAND-PAINTED sign on State Highway 27, a few miles north of Mari Sandoz's grave, reads "Sandoz Books and Museum, 6 miles." A dirt road rolls east through hay meadows and conical dunes and branches off to the right where another sign reads "Caroline Sandoz Pifer, .5 miles."

Caroline Pifer's modern ranch house sits on a hill with a view to the south over some of her ten thousand acres of rolling mixed-grass prairie and subirrigated meadows. A small note taped beside the screen door invites visitors to sit on the porch and enjoy the wildlife. Bird feeders hang from several of the fifty species of trees and shrubs in her garden.

Caroline Pifer, an energetic, independent, gracious, and very funny woman of eighty-some years, invites me in and takes me down to the basement, where Sandoz memorabilia are displayed. After a brief tour, we sit at the kitchen table over coffee discussing topics ranging from pioneer history to the shorebird population decline to cosmology. I ask her what she likes about living in one of the remotest parts of the Sandhills.

"I guess it's what everyone else would hate, but I like the isolation. I enjoy company, but I like to have the next day off."

I am today's company, and our agenda includes a ranch tour. We climb into an old pickup and head off across country with the big bluestem brushing against the hood and the truck rocking from side to side over gopher mounds and other minor obstacles.

"I'd let you drive, but then I'd have to give directions, and it would take too much time," she says, as we top a steep hill and bounce down into a narrow, green valley.

We see a pair of black terns swooping over the bulrushes and two trumpeter swans standing beside a muskrat house.

"I could have this drained and grow some more hay, but I like to keep it this way for the birds."

Caroline Pifer's ranch is one of the finest representatives of native mixed-grass prairie I've ever seen. Only a handful of weeds, few signs of overgrazing, bluestem and switch-grass growing four to six feet tall, red-winged blackbirds, curlews, marsh hawks, and white-tailed deer everywhere. It wasn't always that way, she says. "When Papa first came to this country many of the hills were bare of grass, and there were blowouts everywhere. There was hardly a tree to be seen."

Good stewardship, control of prairie fires, and maybe a little luck with the rain have turned things around. From a hill behind the ranch house, we gaze out over a landscape as green as Ireland. Except that here there are no houses, hardly any fences, and as for people, just the two of us.

As we stand silently on the hilltop, a wave of sadness washes over me. I see images of bulldozers crashing through the orchards on the hillsides behind my childhood home in the Santa Clara Valley; houses and roads gobbling up tallgrass meadows along the Colorado Front Range; hordes of people filling every open space. I wonder how it feels to live in a place where the view from the front porch barely changes during a lifetime, where you can grow and bond with the landscape, where memories, both bitter and sweet, have no place to hide. I wonder how much of our contemporary malaise, our emptiness, stems from this loss of connection.

CAROLINE WAS the youngest of Jules and Mary Sandoz's six children. By the time she was born in 1910, life had begun to soften at the Sandoz ranch. The country was mostly settled. A doctor lived within a couple of miles of the house, and neighbors came almost daily to trade at Old Jules's small store or to pick fruit from his orchard. Saturday night barn dances began at sundown and lasted until dawn.

"We had a real community. We had people within a mile or so in every direction, and there was never a shortage of someone to play with . . . if we had time to play."

I ask if she has any good stories about walking ten miles to school or surviving blizzards, grasshopper plagues, or tornadoes.

"No," she laughs, "It was only a mile and a half to school, and we hardly missed a day during the winter. I'd grab hold of my brother Fritz's coattails, he was seven years older and a long strider, and he'd pull me right through the drifts." There wasn't always a lot to eat, but folks learned young to take advantage of what nature provided. "We were always interested in birds, because for one thing, in the early days that was your food. I can remember going curlew hunting with my brother. . . . Oh, they were delicious! We'd eat them bones and all, they were so tender."

Caroline married Robert Pifer in 1935. They started out with $500, seven head of cattle, a saddle horse, and thirty-three acres of rented farmland. Caroline would walk to her mother's house with a rifle in hand, hoping to meet a cottontail or two.

"Soon there wasn't a rabbit left in the whole country, they'd all been shot and eaten, for nearly everyone not on relief was at least short of money." But, she adds cheerfully, "We didn't mind the depression so much because everyone else was so hard up. When we got married in '35, we didn't have anything, but no one else did either."

By 1943 Robert and Caroline had a small place of their own. They gradually expanded their herds and landholdings, and both grew to love the ranching life. Of her husband, who died from cancer in 1974, Caroline says, "He could spend hours with [his] cattle, admiring. . . . He thought he had everything one could want from life."

An optimist at heart, Caroline Pifer seems like the type of person who could do almost anything—ranching, surviving the depression, teaching, or becoming a writer. When

Mari Sandoz died in 1966, Caroline, as executor of her sister's estate, inherited the task of compiling and publishing hundreds of letters, dozens of unpublished stories and articles, and an unfinished autobiography. To improve her editing and writing skills she went back to school, earning her bachelor of arts degree in English literature at Chadron State College at age seventy-one. Returning to school, which many would have found daunting, was another rich and positive experience.

"It was wonderful. Shakespeare. . . . I'd never experienced Shakespeare, except in high school, and then I didn't really understand him. I had some wonderful teachers. There was so much to learn."

Each summer several score of "Sandoz buffs" visit the small museum in her basement or drop by to chat or to buy a book. In 1987 Caroline wrote a book of her own, a carefully crafted biography of her brother Jules, *Son of Old Jules.* It will be her last.

"When Mari died, someone had to do something. She wanted me to finish her autobiography, but I really didn't want to do it. . . . When I got that book out, *Son of Old Jules,* I discovered I could never write like she did. So I've lost all interest in writing. When I turned eighty, I said, 'This is it, now I can relax.' "

Back at the ranch house we stand in the garden admiring the birds and the wildflowers. Caroline tells stories about a mountain lion bounding through the grass, rattlesnakes as thick as your arm, and hailstones so big they knocked the knotholes out of the wooden boards on her old house. She tells me about her latest project, planting trees in blowouts.

"I get about a 20 percent survival rate, which isn't bad for a blowout. I don't have to water them at all. The blowouts collect the rainwater like a funnel, and it's enough to keep the trees growing."

I tell her about my turkey friend, Roxanne, the avocet convention at Wood Lake, and the river otter I saw in the North Platte that morning. We exchange books. A flock of sharp-tailed grouse fly in and land a few yards away.

"It must be a treat having a threatened species in your front yard."

"They haven't been coming around as much lately. I think one of the neighbors has been feeding them. But they're right on schedule today."

She is smiling broadly, still watching the grouse, as I drive back down the road.

LOST CHOKECHERRY VALLEY

IN THE HEART of the Sandhills lies a sheltered valley where the Northern Cheyenne spent their last winter of freedom. I had longed to go there since reading *Cheyenne Autumn*, Mari Sandoz's fictionalized account of that incredible winter. Lost Chokecherry Valley remains well hidden. Historians still debate the exact location where about 150 Northern Cheyenne holed up for three months while thousands of federal troops searched for them in vain.

The Northern Cheyenne's heroic flight to the Yellowstone River began in Fort Reno, Oklahoma. During spring 1877 they had surrendered to federal troops at Fort Robinson, in northwestern Nebraska. Against the will of most tribal members, the Northern Cheyenne were marched south to "Indian Country" in Oklahoma to await the long-promised provisions, peace, and reservation land.

Before they completed the long journey south, starvation and disease had already begun to decimate the population. By summer 1878 dozens had succumbed to dysentery and fever. When the leaders protested, some were placed in irons and imprisoned. Many of the Cheyenne lost hope. They believed staying would mean dying from alien diseases in alien country. Flight would bring almost certain death at the hands of several thousand federal troops stationed across the western plains.

On a moonlit night in early September, about three hundred Northern Cheyenne, approximately one-fifth of those who remained of the once formidable tribe, slipped out of their camp near Fort Reno and passed silently through the lines of watching soldiers. They left behind most of what they owned: tipis, many horses, their heavier possessions. They walked resolutely, sadly, beginning the long trek toward their ancestral home by the Yellowstone River, eight hundred miles to the north.

As they marched northward, the outnumbered Cheyenne fought engagement after engagement with federal troops— near the Cimarron and the Arkansas and along Frenchman's Creek south of the Platte. Many of the old and infirm dropped out to die on the prairie. Mothers with infants hid in prairie washes and gullies as the troops clattered by.

Iron Teeth, a Cheyenne woman, described the journey during a 1926 interview with journalist and ethnographer Thomas Bailey Marquis:

> Chills and fever kept me sick all along the way. We had not any lodges. At night, when we could make any kind of camp, my daughters helped me at making willow branch shelters. . . .
>
> . . . We dodged the soldiers during most of the way of our long journey. But always they were near us and trying to catch us. Our young men fought them off in seven different battles. At each fight, some of our people were killed, women or children the same as men. I do not know how many of our grown-up people were killed. But I know that more than sixty of our children were gone when we got to the Dakota country.

Near the Sappa River the Cheyenne avenged an earlier massacre at the hands of Union troops by raiding several frontier settlements, slaughtering nineteen whites, and stealing their provisions and horses. News of the "murderous" Cheyenne spread across the country, and more troops rode west.

Somehow the Cheyenne made it across the Platte River, where federal troops had waited for days. But the soldiers were closing in and the situation seemed desperate. A dispute arose. Some, led by the popular old chief Morning Star, split off to the northwest, toward the Sioux agency on the White River. They hoped federal agents would permit them to stay with their Sioux friend Red Cloud while they awaited the long-sought reservation on the Yellowstone.

The others, led by Chief Little Wolf, feared that surrendering to federal agents would only lead to their being forcibly returned to the "country of death" in Oklahoma. But they couldn't go north across the Niobrara. The Black Hills and White River country swarmed with soldiers. They decided to disperse into the dunes, where few soldiers would follow, and meet after a few days in a tiny valley hidden among the maze of hills.

Morning Star's party of about 150, which included Iron Teeth and her family, was soon captured and imprisoned in Fort Robinson. When the captives refused to return south, the commandant denied them food and water. After several days they fled the barracks. The soldiers hunted them down one by one, killing more than sixty men, women, and children.

During the massacre Iron Teeth and her older daughter scrambled up into the limestone cliffs overlooking the White River and crawled into a small cave. They hid there for six days and nights, subsisting on a few ounces of jerky and melted snow. Their toes and fingers froze. They dared not look out, but they could hear gunfire and the cries of the wounded. On the seventh day, a captain who had noticed their tracks leading into the cave called out to them, promising he would not harm them.

Iron Teeth didn't dare ask the soldiers about the fate of her son and youngest daughter. She watched silently as the "soldier doctor" rubbed snow on her frozen extremities. Finally, her little girl came running up to her:

I asked her about her brother. It appeared she did not hear me, so I asked again. This time she burst out crying. Then I knew he had been killed. She told me how it had been done. That night, they had hidden in a deep pit. The next morning, some soldiers had come near to them. The brother had said to her: "Lie down, and I will cover you with leaves and dirt. Then I will climb out and fight the soldiers. They will kill me, but they will think I am the only one here, and they will go away after I am dead. When they are gone, you can come out and hunt for our mother." The next day she came out, but the soldiers caught her.

After the massacre at Fort Robinson, public opinion across the country shifted decidedly in favor of the Cheyenne. While the stragglers were rounded up and more leaders placed in irons, politicians in Washington began to talk seriously about creating a Northern Cheyenne reservation.

Meanwhile Little Wolf's party had vanished. For three months federal troops combed the area south of the Black Hills and north of the Platte. False rumors of Cheyenne sightings were rampant. Settlers reported seeing mounted braves as far west as Box Butte and as far east as Valentine. The local newspapers wrongly blamed marauding Cheyenne for a variety of conflicts, including range wars and random frontier violence.

Had Little Wolf heard these stories, he might have been amused or disgusted. He still wore the silver peace medal given to him by the "white father" in Washington. While the soldiers scurried across the prairie like so many disoriented ants, he and his people were busy surviving, living out their last winter of freedom in the remote little valley.

From their posts high on a ridge top, Cheyenne scouts could see wagon trains inching northward on the Ogallala Trail, far to the east. Below the scouts, Cheyenne women skinned elk, pronghorn, and deer. Cheyenne children played around carefully tended campfires in the box elder and hackberry thickets at the south end of the valley.

Chokecherries, wrinkled from the frost and early snow, dangled from withered branches. A few ducks paddled across a shallow lake. Migrating snow geese made pearl-white Vs against the cerulean autumn sky. When danger approached, fires were extinguished and everyone disappeared into pits dug into the soft sand. At night elders gathered to discuss strategy, while young lovers courted in the light of the rekindled fires.

It was said to be one of the worst autumn-winter seasons on record, with incessant snow and nighttime temperatures dropping to ⁻40 degrees. Many suffered from frostbite. Fortunately the Cheyenne managed to intercept one of the last of the great elk herds that once roamed throughout western Nebraska. The slaughtered elk provided warm robes for everyone, along with elk teeth and horns for adornment and engagement gifts. The elk meat and that of a few stray cattle and horses from nearby ranches kept everyone alive through the coldest part of winter.

Eventually a scout brought back word of the savage treatment of Morning Star's party at the fort. Little Wolf's band decided they could no longer stand by. In late January they left the valley for good, resuming their journey north.

They finally capitulated in March, huddling exhausted and near starvation along the Powder River, seventy-five miles south of the Yellowstone. Little Wolf surrendered to Lieutenant W. P. "White Hat" Clark, who reputedly told him, "Now I have found my friend Little Wolf, I am glad. I have been anxious to see you. You will not be harmed."

Only 114 people remained of the nearly 300 who had begun the journey six months before. Back at Fort Robinson, more Cheyenne leaders were arrested and shipped off to prison. Five years later, the government granted the Northern Cheyenne their tiny reservation on the Tongue River in southeastern Montana.

Iron Teeth described her feelings to Thomas Marquis forty-seven years later:

> I used to cry every time anything reminded me of the killing of my husband and my son. But now I have become old enough to talk quietly of them. I used to hate all white people, especially their soldiers. But my heart now has become changed to softer feelings. Some of the white people are good, maybe as good as Indians.
>
> According to our ways, it is considered not right to speak the name of any of our own dead relatives. But mine have been gone many years, and you are well known to us, so I have told you who was my husband. I tell you now the name of my son who was killed: we called him

Mon-see-yo-mon—Gathering His Medicine. Lots of times, as I sit here alone on the floor with my blanket wrapped about me, I lean forward and close my eyes and think of him standing up out of the pit and fighting the soldiers, knowing that he would be killed, but doing this so that his little sister might get away into safety. Don't you think he was a brave young man?

As a child Mari Sandoz heard of the lost valley south of the Niobrara and longed to visit it, but none of her Sandhills neighbors could tell her where to look. While researching *Cheyenne Autumn*, Mari spent several weeks on the Northern Cheyenne reservation. She gained the confidence of an elder named Old Cheyenne Woman, who recounted detailed stories of that fall and winter of 1878–79. A Cheyenne man gave her a map of the valley and described its approximate location. Mari and a friend flew back and forth over the Sandhills until they found the place depicted on the map.

The valley they identified as Lost Chokecherry lay only a few miles north of the ranch where Mari Sandoz spent her teenage years, the Sandoz home place south of Gordon. Although some historians suggested a more southerly location for Little Wolf's winter camp, Mari was certain she had found the site. In every respect it matched the descriptions provided by her Cheyenne informants, "a valley so small and sheltered," she wrote, "it seemed held within the cupping of two warm palms."

When Mari's sister, Caroline Pifer, gave me directions to this valley, she said the place sent a chill down her spine. I asked if her feelings had anything to do with spirits or with the traditional Cheyenne belief that what once happens in a place is always happening there. "No," she said, "I don't believe in spirits or anything like that. It's just thinking of what went on there. It was so incredible."

ON A BLUSTERY afternoon in late April, I follow a cattle trail up over a low rise and down into a small horseshoe-shaped hollow tucked into the high hills south of the Niobrara River. I pause on a grassy bench and take a long look. Down to the left lies a sky blue lake, alive with the quacking of mallards, gadwalls, and pintails. Beyond the lake the valley opens out eastward onto a sea of saffron hills. Cold shadows wash over the closed end, where the dunes rise more steeply.

As I make my way down toward the water, three white-tailed deer bound out of the darkness and streak off over a sunlit ridge. A Swainson's hawk screams from her nest atop a half-dead hackberry, while two downy white heads peer out over the edge. Her alarm cries blend with the wails of curlews and the riotous exclamations of the ducks, geese, and yellow-headed blackbirds down in the marsh.

Things don't appear to have changed much since the days when the Cheyenne and Lakota hunted in these hills. There are a few cattle trails zigzagging across the hillsides, a round stock tank near the lakeshore, and some deciduous trees probably planted by early settlers. But native hackberries and box elders still darken the north-facing dunes, and it's easy to discern the small clearing, described in *Cheyenne Autumn*, where the Cheyenne were said to have built their evening fires and held council. Nearby, a handful of scrawny chokecherry bushes cling to the sandy soil.

I walk across a steep, sandy hillside and continue up through a narrow pass leading off into the heaving, russet hills to the west. The wind, which has blown hard from the north for two days, dies to a whisper. A full moon eases its way up into the pale turquoise sky. Silver reflections dance on the gently rippling water. A willet cries "pee-wee-wee, pee-wee-wee" over and over.

The couple who manage the ranch invited me to spend the night in the valley. It's a tempting offer, but it doesn't seem like the right thing to do. This peaceful place seems better left to spirit and memory. But before I leave, I pause at the crest of the highest hill to listen one last time.

Now the only sounds are the low murmur of the night breeze and the eerie "winnowing" of two common snipes performing their courtship flights at opposite ends of the lake. As the snipes dive and the wind whistles through their tail feathers, the tremulous notes float out over the water and melt away into the moonlit hills. The winnowing seems melancholy and vaguely dissonant, like the high trilling of Cheyenne women signaling the end of a painful journey.

NIGHT

It is there that our hearts are set,
In the expanse of the heavens.

—Pawnee song

SOMEWHERE ALONG the way, most of us lost contact with the night. This alienation must have begun when we discovered fire and learned to build shelters, and it no doubt intensified during the Industrial Revolution when gas and electricity enabled us to exclude the darkness from our lives. For whatever reason, we are becoming a species that experiences only half of life, retaining little knowledge of that mystical period between sunset and sunrise. Few among us can name more than a handful of constellations, distinguish the scream of a frightened owl from the cry of a wounded rabbit, or walk confidently through the woods on a moonless night.

The people who lived on the periphery of the Sand-hills before white settlement would have found this ignorance of the darkness baffling. To the Pawnee, the stars were a road map guiding every action. The stars' positions told when to plant corn, when to harvest, when to hunt. At night, visions came floating on the still air, bringing guidance, reassurance, and connection with the ancient ones.

In Lakota religion every object has a spirit, and every spirit is *wakan*, meaning sacred or beyond normal human consciousness. Spirits appear most frequently at night, when ghosts of dead relatives may materialize in the form of an owl or some other nocturnal creature. The campfires of departed ones blaze high overhead along the Path of Souls, known today as the Milky Way, the trail to the final spirit resting place. To walk under the stars is to walk among the spirits, the ancestors, all that is holy.

On traditional vision quests, Lakota men deprive themselves of food and water while sitting alone for four days and four nights. The spirits generally put in an appearance by the third or fourth night. These spirits, sometimes reassuring, sometimes terrifying, strip away falseness and pretension, exposing the quester's soul to whatever lurks out there in the void. Shaman Wallace Black Elk writes: "I'm scared when that spirit comes. Don't think I'm standing there with my hands on my hips or banging my chest saying, 'Come here, I want to talk to you. What's this, what's that.' I'm not inquisitive. I just humble myself. The spirit is the master. He could do anything, and you'll never know what he'll do."

I FEEL THE summer night descending on Pine Lake about an hour before sunset. The afternoon breeze subsides, and a pleasant coolness settles in. The green hills begin to glow in the soft evening light, while the lake turns a deeper shade of blue. A phalanx of crows flap by, cawing in chorus as they approach their roost in the pines.

I walk down to the cattail marsh at the north end of the lake, where marsh wrens chatter and yellow-headed blackbirds gurgle and rasp while clinging to swaying cattail stalks. As the sun sinks toward the horizon, the surface of the inlet rocks gently to a standstill. Water striders skate out from shore, dragging their reflections behind them. A pied-billed grebe clucks nervously while cruising through the cattails with four fluffy young clinging to her back.

The deep voice of a male great horned owl booms out across the water. The female's quavering contralto answers a moment later, followed by the hoots of another pair in the cottonwoods far to the east. The nearby pair hoots in synchrony, first the male, "wh-whoo, whoo-whooo," then the female, "wh-wh-whoo, wh-whoo-who," then the male again, monotonously, over and over, until dusk settles in.

As I listen to the owls' commanding voices, it's easy to imagine they're speaking to me. I once startled a Lakota acquaintance by telling her I was planning to go out calling owls with a tape recorder. "You don't want to do that," she said. Plains Indian tradition holds that hooting owls may be departed spirits returning to claim the souls of the living.

In Cheyenne the word *mistai* means both "owl" and "spirit." One Cheyenne story tells of a family that almost freezes to death when a *mistai* living near their lodge kills everyone who ventures out to get water or gather firewood. In another story, an owl ghost makes off with a small child.

In Lakota tradition the great horned owl is also described as a keeper-of-game spirit that watches over the bison. The burrowing owl can act as a protective spirit. Warriors who wear its feathers or carry a live owl with them cannot be injured in battle.

The qualities that give owls their magical aura—their hypnotic calls, silent flight, and piercing gaze—enable them to dominate the night. Loud hoots keep competitors away from hunting areas. Their large round eyes and oversized, widely spaced ears allow owls to see clearly in the dark and hear a mouse rustling at four hundred yards. Silent flight helps them to appear and vanish at will.

Spirits or no, they cast a potent spell. The Pine Lake owls know exactly where I am and what I'm doing at any moment. When I come to the lake they perch in the pines above my tent and hoot me to sleep. They may be asserting territorial rights, checking out the newcomer, or hunting mice scurrying among the picnic leavings, but I take it as a form of welcome.

While studying northern pygmy-owls in the foothills

west of Boulder, Colorado, I learned how adept owls are at recognizing individual humans. After I found their nest in a woodpecker hole in a large ponderosa pine, the pygmy-owl adults harassed me whenever I came by. It didn't matter if I wore different clothes or averted my gaze. I could sit on a rock two hundred yards away and the owls would perch above my head and twitter in alarm while ignoring other hikers, including those right under their nest tree.

I believe the Pine Lake owls have a similar ability to "remember faces," and that is why they follow me around. I have seen their nest on several occasions, so I am part of their inner circle—an old acquaintance and a potential enemy.

After the owls stop hooting, I stroll through the woods listening for the distinctive hisses and rasps their young make when begging for food. I find the family in a grove of pines about fifty yards back from the campground. At the base of an excrement-splattered trunk lie dozens of owl pellets, oblong masses of regurgitated bones and fur. I settle into the soft pine needles and gaze up. Something scrambles from one branch to another. A gut-wrenching wail and three harsh barks pierce the night. "If you say so," I whisper, and leave them to their conjuring.

WITH CRICKETS chirruping, fireflies flashing, and a mother lode of stars blazing overhead, I can barely feel my feet touch the ground as I walk along the sandy road bordering the lake. The wavering firefly light creates a sense of motion, making the starlit landscape dip and roll like a ship at sea.

The fireflies concentrate in flooded meadows adjacent to the marsh. In early summer the males switch on their abdominal luminescence display to attract willing females. A male flutters a few feet above the ground, inscribing an incendiary arc, announcing, "I am a male of firefly species X, and I am ready to mate." A second or two later a short flash answers from ground level, "I am a female of your species. Come here and let's consider mating." Sometimes the female turns out to be a large-bodied impostor of another species that has broken the male's code and will have him for dinner. Most of the time the system works.

Biologists say you can attract males by lying on the ground and flicking a penlight on and off. I avoid this practice. It would break the spell, and it seems as unfair as hunting ducks with a howitzer. Besides, the meadow is dank, and the female mosquitoes would have *me* for dinner.

Fireflies, or lightning bugs, are beetles in the family Lampyridae. As larvae they live on the ground under bark or leaves; most feed on small invertebrates, including snails and slugs. They kill their prey by crunching down with their powerful mandibles, injecting a poison, and sucking out the insides. The adults spend much of their lives searching for mates. After mating, the female lays a clump of eggs on the ground or on low vegetation. The eggs and larvae of many species glow with an eerie yellow green luminescence.

How did something as exotic as fireflies end up in this sea of sand? They may be holdovers from the last ice age, when forests and swamps covered much of the region; or they may have made their way westward to this wetland along the same route followed by early white explorers.

Such an exodus would require many firefly generations, but for the sake of visualizing the remoteness of this colony, it's instructive to imagine a single male making the journey. He sets out from the lower Mississippi River Valley, among dense forests of oak, birch, and maple. Around St. Louis he signals for a left turn up the Missouri. Here the valley forest remains lush and humid, but meadows of swaying Indian grass and big bluestem carpet the uplands. After a few hundred miles he veers west again, following the Niobrara into the Sandhills. The deciduous forest thins to a narrow strip on each side of the river, and isolated groves of ponderosa pine darken the canyon walls. All else is grass, stretching endlessly in every direction. Finally, 250 miles up the Niobrara, he turns south along five-foot-wide Pine Creek. He follows this meandering brook across the prairie for thirty miles, flitting from one saturated meadow to another until he reaches the marsh where I now stand.

The water that feeds the marsh flows from an immense aquifer, but the marsh ecosystem is connected to similar habitat by a trickle of water. Given a few hours and a bulldozer, a person could divert the flow of Pine Creek, leaving the fireflies, the willows, and other moisture-loving creatures isolated from the primeval forest where they evolved.

Many of the fireflies at Pine Lake belong to the genus *Photuris*, a complex group that ranges throughout much of North America. Members of this genus tend to look identical, and species recognition was all but impossible until the 1940s when scientists began documenting differences in the flashing patterns of *Photuris* males. Each species has a slightly different signature. Some emit short, intense greenish white flashes; others, lingering orange flashes. Some species flash in J patterns, others in dots, zigzags, or sine waves.

Documenting firefly flash patterns is no easy task. The ephemeral firefly light barely pierces our reality, vanishing just as we take note of it. In my night photographs, the fireflies are no more visible than any of the other *wakan* spirits.

While walking along the road, I stalk a flashing beetle and snare it with my hand. It flutters in my palm for a few seconds and then settles down in the flashlight beam, half an inch long, brown and yellow, with long, dusky wings and a square, armored head.

The firefly floats away in slow motion, like a feather riding on the night breeze. I track its flashes across the marsh until they mingle with hundreds of others.

ABOUT MIDNIGHT an emissary from the Rocky Mountains comes visiting. At first I note a faint flickering and an almost subliminal rumbling. Soon the flashes grow bright enough to illuminate the landscape for a microsecond. I count the intervals. One one thousand, two one thousand. . . . "Craaack!" A brief silence. Another flash, more intense. One one thou— . . . "Boom!!!" Everything shakes, and the air crackles. The lightning bolts explode in quick succession, making images of the lake and surrounding hills flicker on and off like pictures in a magic lantern show. The rain comes in bursts and passes quickly.

These midnight thunderstorms, born from the mixing of hot and cold air as the sun beats down on the Medicine Bow Range two hundred miles to the west, have usually lost much of their punch by the time they reach the Sandhills. Nevertheless, this particular thunder and lightning display is plenty terrifying, and it's a relief to feel that last whoosh of wind, the cool outflow of the receding thunderhead, as the storm passes to the east.

With the cooling of the air the mosquitoes grow too lethargic to bite and the crickets chirp languidly, as if sedated. I lie in the moist sand gazing up at the constellations—the Summer Triangle overhead, red Antares on the southern horizon, and the Big Dipper suspended above the pines. I get up and wander off toward the North Star.

On the sandy bank beside the dirt road, evening primroses have opened their creamy blossoms to receive the evening sacrament. It is to be delivered by a snowberry clearwing, a long-tongued sphinx moth (also known as a hummingbird moth) that inserts its proboscis into the flower's narrow throat to extract the sweet nectar. In doing so the moth rubs against the flower's stamens, and the dusty yellow pollen sticks to its head and body. When the moth flies to another flower, the pollen brushes against the flower's style and makes its way down the pistil to the ovary. The following morning the flower's petals fold up and wither away. Come evening, new buds will unfurl to embrace the darkness and patiently await the moth's arrival.

Had I walked by this place at midday, I might not have noticed the plants at all. The pale evening primrose grows low to the ground, and its flower buds are an inconspicuous dull green. A few hours before sunset the buds spring into action, requiring only minutes to stretch, snap, and fully extend their crinkly white petals. This rapid unfolding creates an almost embarrassing sense of intimacy. There's life here, a form of consciousness yearning to create more life.

Now the evening primroses and I wait for the moth, but no moth appears. A few crickets chirp drowsily. All else is stillness, an inky void filled with who knows what. In the movies, night scenes are accompanied by a continuous racket: owls hooting, dogs and wolves baying, poorwills poorwilling. But what really gives the night its character is the silence. With little to see or hear, sensory deprivation allows consciousness to drift into uncharted spaces.

"Eoeeeerr . . . eoeeeerr . . . eoeeeerr. . . . " A synthetic, piercing wail comes from the pines behind the campground. I follow it through the woods, but it stays just ahead of me, first on my right, then on my left. Pine needles crackle and something scurries by. I stumble and fall to my knees. The wailing continues, somewhere in the pines ahead. I reach the edge of the woods. Nothing. "Eoeeeerr. . . . Eoeeeerr. . . ."

Now it's behind me, coming from the place I was standing moments before. I give up and sit in the sand, listening, until the exquisite screaming dies away. More conjuring.

I lay my sleeping bag on the grass beside the picnic tables and crawl in. Silence mingles with foggy consciousness. The earth turns a few degrees toward dawn.

I yawn, stretch, and check my bearings. The Big Dipper has wheeled around to the north, and Antares has dropped out of sight. A half-moon hangs over the eastern horizon. I get up, walk down the road, and kneel among the evening primroses.

A shadowy form flits from flower to flower on gently whirring wings. I hold out my hand, but the moth appears to fly right through it. I try to slow the scene down, to see things one instant at a time.

Through half-closed eyes I finally follow the moth's flight as it dives into the milky folds of a waiting blossom. It emerges seconds later, its fuzzy head dripping nectar and its dusky wings spewing a cloud of golden pollen. When I open my eyes fully the moth is gone and the pollen no more visible than grains of stardust.

> In the great night my heart will go out;
> Toward me the darkness comes rattling.
> In the great night my heart will go out.
>
> —Papago

PLUMS IN THE WATER

We Hidatsa raise corn, beans, sunflower seed, and good squashes to eat. We are not starving that we must eat rose berries. . . . We think they are food for wild men.

—from a traditional Hidatsa story

WHAT BETTER way to absorb the flavor of the country than to spend three days in the Sandhills subsisting on wild foods? To avoid eating something harmful, I arm myself with two field guides. Bradford Angier's wildly enthusiastic *Field Guide to Edible Wild Plants* came out during the height of the back-to-nature movement of the 1970s. Angier never met a wild plant he didn't like. However, a cautionary note in Angier's book warns that the publishers "assume no responsibility for adverse health effects" from eating foods the author recommends.

Kelly Kindscher's more comprehensive and conservative *Edible Wild Plants of the Prairie* lists more than eighty edible prairie plants, although Kindscher points out that many of them are toxic or barely palatable. Just to be safe, I carry along two six-packs of Newcastle Brown Ale to use as a palliative in case of emergency.

It's early August, and the prairie blushes with color after a mild, wet summer. I start out at Long Lake, in the eastern Sandhills where such delicacies as wild rice and prairie turnips grow, and work my way westward, sampling everything I can positively identify.

August 3, Long Lake

With great horned owls hooting, western kingbirds and goldfinches chirping away, and the sun an orange ball on the misty horizon, I wander up toward the grassy uplands at the west end of the lake. In the marsh beside the lakeshore I gather some rose hips for tea, harvest arrowhead roots for a stew, and strip protein-rich pollen from the cattail stalks. I cut several cattail stalks at the base, scooping out the celery-like pulp, and collect some fresh peppermint for flavoring.

While gathering milkweed pods for my stew, I come across a pair of monarch butterflies linked back to back at the tips of their abdomens. In a couple of months these monarchs' offspring will begin their migration to Michoacán in central Mexico and other points south. Milkweed toxins stored in their bodies make the migration possible. Birds that eat these brightly colored butterflies get sick and learn to avoid them. The monarchs ride the autumn breezes southward, carrying the residue of their milkweed hosts along as an insurance policy.

The puffy, crescent-shaped milkweed pods contain a pale green pulp. In late summer the pulp matures into dozens of hard black seeds, each attached to a plume of silky hairs. When the pods ripen and open, these silk parachutes catch the wind, which disperses the seeds for miles. Plains Indian children played with the dried pods and seeds, and white settlers used the silk to stuff pillows and mattresses.

The uplands around Long Lake yield leadplant for tea, Rocky Mountain bee plant for a potherb, and some juniper berries for flavoring. The prairie turnips have long since lost their purple blossoms and disappeared in the sea of green.

BRUNCH

Cattail Pollen Porridge with Juniper Berries
Rose Tea

The less said about this gooey concoction the better. But both cattails and junipers (also called red cedar) contributed substantially to Plains Indian life. The Pawnee used cattail down to make dressings for burns, to protect infants from chafing, and to fill pillows. The Lakota boiled juniper berries and twigs to make a decoction for coughs. During the cholera epidemic of 1849–50 this decoction was said to have saved many lives. The Lakota also tied juniper boughs to tipi poles to ward off lightning, and they placed juniper twigs on the hot stones in the sweat lodge during purification rituals.

Osage mythology referred to the juniper as the tree of life, home to the thunderbirds that guarded the sacred path to the west and brought violent storms to the prairie. Some Lakota holy men say that if you stand under a juniper during a thunderstorm, the lightning will never strike you.

SUPPER

Milkweed Pod and Arrowhead Root Stew
Heart of Cattail Salad with Salsify Root
Leadplant Tea

The toxins in milkweed plants, called cardiac glycosides, are poisonous to humans as well as to birds. Even with the more "edible" species you have to boil the pods several times, changing the water after each boiling, to remove the toxins. Unfortunately this leaves the pods with a slimy consistency that makes okra seem crunchy by comparison. The leadplant tea looks golden and exudes a smoky aroma reminiscent of Lapsang souchong.

Kindscher praises milkweed as one of the most nutritious and versatile of wild prairie foods. The Omaha and Pawnee called cabbage "white man's milkweed." The Osage ate the tender milkweed sprouts, the flower buds, and the young fruit pods. The Crow Indians ate milkweed seeds and made a weak syrup from dew collected from the fragrant flowers.

August 4, Pine Lake

A gentle trilling outside the tent interrupts my dreams. Roxanne is busy cleaning up the remains of the previous camping party's supper. She looks at me beseechingly.

"If you get any fatter, the coyotes will get you for sure."
She responds with a few seductive clucks, and I toss her a
handful of cattail pollen, which she ignores. We stroll off
into the hills around the lake.

Taking a wild turkey along on a foraging expedition is
like going on a manhunt with a bloodhound. The hills are
alive with edibles: seeds, wildflowers, grubs, grasshoppers,
beetles—you name it. Unfortunately, few of these items appeal to my urban-adapted palate, so I settle for some gooseberries, some large, ripe rose hips, a few prickly pear pads
and fruits, wild mint, and more bee plant. I decide to forgo
the milkweed, but I strip some cattail pollen for pancakes
and harvest some cattail shoots for a salad. While Roxanne
wanders off into the woods, I return to camp to sip on a
bottle of brown ale.

BRUNCH

Pancakes Made from Cattail Pollen, Rose Hips, and
    Bee Plant
Topping of Fresh Gooseberries
Peppermint Tea

SUPPER

Prickly Pear and Wild Onion Stew
Prickly Pear Fruits
Bee Plant Tea and Rose Tea
Fresh Chokecherries

What extraordinary pancakes! To prepare them I mix the
pollen with a few teaspoons of water, some crushed rose

hips, and the steamed bee plant leaves, which taste a lot like Swiss chard. Then I pat the mixture into cakes and fry them in some contraband salad oil. It's important to use the cattail pollen, which grows at the end of the stalk, and not the seeds (the conspicuous, cylindrical part of the stalk). The cactus stew proves even less tasty and more glutinous than the milkweed version. I spend a good fifteen minutes removing microscopic prickly pear thorns from my fingers.

Chokecherries are an acquired taste. When eaten raw their astringency makes my mouth pucker. After the first frost, when dried chokecherries shrivel up like raisins on the vine, they lose much of their bite. It's pleasant to munch on these dried berries while wandering over the hills looking for bison or other signs of lost civilizations, or while exercising your turkey.

Plains Indians coveted chokecherries. They mashed them up and mixed them with bison fat to make pemmican, a winter staple, or crushed them to make a special drink. Many peoples referred to the August moon as the "black cherry moon" or "the moon of black cherries ripening." The Lakota drank chokecherry juice at ceremonies honoring a girl reaching puberty. The red juice represented both the sacred blood of the young woman and the fruits of the earth.

Plains Indian tribes would camp for days along streams where chokecherries grew. The women used stone pestles to pound the cherries to a pulp, pits and all. It's possible that people deliberately carried chokecherry seeds from one campsite to another, contributing to the spread of this moisture-loving shrub into arid regions.

With all the emphasis historians have placed on the Plains Indians' association with bison, it's easy to forget how important plants were to these peoples. Before acquiring the horse and rifle during the seventeenth and eighteenth centuries, many plains tribes probably relied on cultivated crops and wild plants for the bulk of their diets. About 60 percent of current U.S. crop production, on a dollar basis, comes from crops first cultivated by Native Americans.

The list of wild foods eaten by the Pawnee, Cheyenne, and Lakota, who lived on the periphery of the Sandhills, equals the inventory of a typical supermarket produce section. It includes serviceberries, hog peanuts, groundnuts, milkweed, hazelnuts, pincushion and prickly pear cactus, wild strawberries, sunflowers, Jerusalem artichokes, groundcherries, wild plums, chokecherries, prairie turnips, buffaloberries, and a plethora of wild grains.

In *Food Plants of the North American Indians*, Elias Yanovsky describes 1,112 species of plants used as food in North America. The relatively moist Sandhills valleys nourished wild plants typical of eastern deciduous forests, including groundnuts and hazelnuts, along with western species such as prickly pear and Rocky Mountain bee plant. Sand cherries and other Sandhills specialists added to the variety.

Finding and collecting wild plants was serious business. In early summer women would mark locations where

Jerusalem artichokes and other tuberous plants grew, so they could return in the fall to harvest the roots when their starch content was highest. Women raided nests of harvest mice for hog peanuts, also known as ground beans. The Omaha planned their early summer bison hunts to pass through regions where prairie turnips were known to grow.

Embedded in the mythology of each Plains Indian tribe are stories of how the people shifted from a plant-based economy to one based on wild game. A tale recounted by Karl Schlesier in *The Wolves of Heaven* tells of the time when the Cheyenne first came to the tallgrass country west of the Mississippi.

Two young shamans were sent out to scout for food. After many days of travel and hardship, they came to a lake at the base of a blue mountain. Nearly starving, they decided to die together on the mountain.

While they were crossing the lake, a water serpent seized the younger man and dragged him under. He struggled for his life as his companion continued on toward the mountain.

Out of nowhere came a strange man wearing a red wolf skin on his head and back. The wolf man dived into the water and killed the serpent. Then he instructed the older shaman to climb the peak.

"You will see there a big rock, which is a door. There you will find an old woman. Tell her that grandfather has killed the serpent he has so long been trying to get."

The shaman soon returned to the lake accompanied by the old woman. They and the wolf man butchered the serpent and carried the young shaman to the mountain door. Once inside, the wolf man and the old woman held a sweat lodge ritual for the dying young man. Within minutes he was completely healed.

As the two men relaxed by the fire, a beautiful young woman walked into the chamber. Wolf man asked, "Do you want to take this woman for your sister, or would one of you wish to marry her?" The younger man agreed to take her as his wife.

As they stood at the cave entrance, the young shamans began to see animals in the four directions. When they and the spirit daughter started out toward their village, they looked behind them and saw thousands of bison and other animals streaming from the mountains. Plants sprouted all around, and a gentle rain began to fall. The earth shone with new freshness.

In this way the Cheyenne were welcomed to their new home in the grasslands and given the right to hunt the animals that lived there.

A century or two later, a new four-legged creature appeared on the prairie. By making bison hunting easier, the horse enabled Plains Indians to become even less dependent on cultivated crops and wild plants, but its acquisition also may have accelerated the downfall of Plains Indian culture. Some historians now believe that bison were on their way to extinction before white hunters began annihilating the herds during the mid-nineteenth century. Most bison had been driven from what is now eastern Nebraska by 1820 as tribes in that region traded hides for guns, utensils, cloth, and food. This trading of bison hides encouraged Plains Indians to turn from a subsistence economy to a more exploitative one and left them more dependent on European American culture and economy.

After eliminating the bison, nineteenth-century white settlers introduced European-style farming to the High Plains. But this imported system fared poorly in an arid environment. When crops failed during the drought years of the 1890s, near-starving settlers turned to many of the same native plants that had nourished Plains Indians for centuries.

Today some Sandhills residents still scour the countryside each summer and fall for chokecherries, wild plums, buffaloberries, and other wild fruits to make into pies and jams. The Sandhills region remains one of the few parts of the country where most residents can name the native plants growing outside their doors. Meanwhile cattle take the place of bison, and the economy is about as stable as it was three hundred years ago.

August 5, Pine Lake

I wake up feeling healthy, euphoric, and hungry. Although the natural foods in my system provide a soothing link with the prairie around me, my stomach feels deprived, and I'm down to two bottles of brown ale. For brunch I heat up some peppermint tea, leadplant tea, and rose hip tea and down a handful of gooseberries. Then I spend the morning reading, relaxing, and listening to the internal grumblings.

The afternoon turns sticky hot, and I have no energy for foraging. Taking my cue from Thoreau, who frequently dined out with friends during his sojourn at Walden Pond, I hop into the car and head for Hyannis.

The old Hyannis Hotel sits on a picturesque main street that climbs up a steep hill off Highway 2. Blink twice and you miss it. But people come from miles around for (with apologies to Roxanne) the fried chicken. I walk through the dreary, deserted bar and into the dining room. A very large man with dark, brooding eyes glares at me from behind the cash register.

"Are you serving supper?"

No response. After what seems like minutes, he points me toward a table in the corner. I'm the only customer, and not a particularly welcome one at that. But I'm so hungry I don't really care.

SUPPER

Fried Chicken
Baked Potato with Sour Cream
Rolls and Butter
Pasta Salad
Three-Bean Salad
Tossed Salad with Blue Cheese Dressing
Radishes and Olives
Apple Pie à la Mode

A Cheyenne story, related by George Grinnell, tells how Wihio, the trickster, was walking along the river and saw dozens of ripe plums down in the water. He said, "Good; there are many plums down there, and I can get all I want."

Wihio took off his clothes and dived in. He felt around for the plums as long as he could hold his breath, but he couldn't find them. As he crawled back up on the bank and again saw the plums in the water, he said to himself, "I must have dived in the wrong place."

Wihio dived and dived, but still he couldn't find the plums. So he got a heavy stone and tied it around his neck and jumped in again. After several minutes of thrashing around under the water, he finally managed to get free of the stone and drag himself up the bank. As he lay there on his back, gasping for breath, he looked up and saw a bush full of ripe plums. But now he was too tired to pick them.

Or, apparently, to drive to Hyannis.

RIFFRAFF

The buffalo will disappear, at last, and another animal will take its place, a slick animal with a long tail and split hooves, whose flesh you will learn to eat. . . . Your ways will change. You will leave your religion for something new. You will lose respect for your leaders and start quarreling with one another. . . . You will take after the Earth Men's ways and forget good things by which you have lived and in the end become worse than crazy.

—words attributed to Sweet Medicine,
Cheyenne culture hero

AFTER A morning spent slogging through brackish, leech-infested water in a futile effort to photograph marsh wrens and rails, I decide to kick back for a while and watch the world go by. I lay my sleeping pad on the mowed grass of the Pine Lake campground and train my telephoto lens on a silver-barked, half-dead cottonwood. Over a period of three hours, two dozen birds come to visit.

One of the first is Roxanne, the camp turkey, skulking through the camping area searching for table scraps. She warbles her familiar high trill and eyes me cautiously while pecking away at the detritus scattered around the picnic tables. Meanwhile yellow-headed blackbirds scramble up the tree trunk gleaning mosquitoes, while an eastern kingbird makes aerial sorties from her perch on a dead limb. Way up in the canopy, yellow warblers, common yellowthroats, warbling vireos, and American goldfinches sing breathlessly as they flutter from one swaying branch to another.

A red-headed woodpecker pokes her head out of a small hole halfway up the trunk. Every few minutes her mate flies in, and they exchange raspy greetings as he stuffs her beak full of insects. Red-headed woodpeckers have been nesting in this same tree for years, raising their young in the protected cavity overlooking the lakeshore.

This year things have changed. A couple of European starlings, a rarity in this part of the Sandhills, have their eyes on the same hole. When the male woodpecker flies off to forage, the starlings poke their beaks into the hole, squawking and fussing, until finally the female woodpecker flies away and a female starling sits in her place.

More likely than not, the starlings will eventually win this battle. Clever opportunists that thrive in a variety of environments, they often displace other cavity nesting birds and occasionally eat their young. Not that red-headed woodpeckers themselves are above such conduct. In *Life Histories of North American Woodpeckers*, Arthur Cleveland Bent referred to these woodpeckers as "murderers and cannibals" for their habit of eating the eggs and young of other species.

Nevertheless, when it comes to wreaking havoc on other North American species, starlings have few equals. The pair in the cottonwood trace their ancestry to around sixty of their kind that were released in New York's Central Park in 1890 by members of the American Acclimatization Society. According to the popular story, these folks wanted to ensure that all the birds mentioned in Shakespeare's plays could be found in North America. They succeeded beyond their wildest dreams. Now more than 200 million starlings infest our cities and forests, gathering in great dark flocks and whistling their squeaky, mynah-like imitations of everything that flies or walks.

Starlings probably have contributed to nationwide declines of a number of native species, including wood ducks, red-headed woodpeckers, and eastern bluebirds. The problem is, who wants to eradicate them, and how? For most of us it's a lot easier to pull weeds than to shoot or poison starlings. Furthermore, schemes to eradicate troublesome birds rarely succeed. For decades midwestern farmers regularly dynamited crow roosts, killing thousands of the crop-eating birds at a time, without making an appreciable dent in regional populations.

The European starling is one of myriad human-associate species that follow us almost everywhere we go. Raccoons, house mice, great horned owls, blue jays, cockroaches, Canada thistle, and cheatgrass also fit comfortably into this category. These opportunists take hold wherever we disturb the natural order: the mammals and birds in cities and rural settlements, the weeds along roads and trails and in over-grazed pastures.

Carhenge, a tongue-in-cheek replica of the Neolithic landmark, sprouts from a winter wheat field a mile north of Alliance. This full-sized reproduction of Stonehenge was constructed of junked automobiles during a family reunion a couple of decades ago. Now it supports possibly the largest house sparrow nesting colony in western Nebraska. The drab little finches, another European export to the New World, chirp and chatter as they stuff nesting material salvaged from the car seats into nooks and crannies in the rusting monoliths.

Only a few nonnative birds have penetrated the periphery of the Sandhills, however. Of the ninety or so species that nest at Pine Lake, only two, the ring-necked pheasant and the starling, are not native to the Great Plains, and both are uncommon at the lake. Few natural areas on the plains can claim this degree of breeding-bird purity.

On the whole, weed species have not fared nearly so well in the Sandhills as in surrounding environments. Whereas knapweed ravages much of Montana and cheatgrass and ragweed infest shortgrass prairies in parts of western Nebraska, the Sandhills prairie remains almost natural. At the Niobrara Valley Preserve east of Valentine, Nature Conservancy staff seeded native grasses on several hundred acres previously tilled for corn and wheat. Within ten years the native grasses dominated the site, and weeds were scattered.

To spread, many weeds need vectors of disturbance such as roads, trails, denuded hillsides, contaminated seed mixes, and people's socks or pets. In the Sandhills the number of vectors has held steady or diminished slightly, and many weed species have kept to the periphery. Still, you can see them—the cheatgrass, timothy, sweet alyssum, fanweed, ragweed, Canada thistle, goosefoot, alfalfa, sweet clover, woolly plantain—encroaching into wetlands, road cuts, old homesteads, and overgrazed hillsides. In a world where everything is becoming homogenized, where flowers, fruit, and pets are daily flown in from every continent and little effort is made to differentiate the native from the exotic, how long can this prairie island hold out?

BEYOND THE grove of junipers and ponderosa pines that shelters Pine Lake from westerly winds, a single pagoda-shaped dune rides several feet above the prevailing chop. From the summit I can see for miles in every direction. To the south, horses and cattle graze amid an elysian tapestry of greening willows and multihued grasses. To the east lies Pine Lake with its rafts of ducks, flotilla of white pelicans, and surrounding ring of cottonwoods and willows. To the north, Pine Creek weaves a serpentine path through the jumble of steep-sided dunes separating Pine Lake from the Niobrara River Valley. Looking westward, it's trough and swell, shadow and sunlight, all the way to the edge of the earth.

From my perch atop the dune I feel safe, insulated from the craziness out there—the bulldozing, strip development, and general mayhem beyond the horizon. But a swarm of alien elements is poised on the perimeter, ready to storm this island of calm. Along the shores of the lake, fields of non-native smooth brome, bluegrass, and timothy flourish in the wet soil. Overhead, seeds of Canada thistle sail by, looking for a spot of bare ground to colonize. Tumbleweeds of Russian thistle and winged pigweed cling to the barbed-wire fences. At Carhenge, an expeditionary force of house sparrows prepares to push out into the hills. Somewhere in Canada, Japan, or the United States, a millionaire gazes at a map of western Nebraska and dreams of golf courses, retirement communities, or massive water diversion projects.

Mustered against these forces of darkness are the sand, resistant to the plow and to some weeds; the aquifer, which helps keep the natural vegetative cover from drying out and blowing away; and a few hundred family ranchers who have looked out for their own interests for over a hundred years, protecting the land from overgrazing and inappropriate development.

More than five hundred square miles of Sandhills prairie lies in federally protected wildlife refuges and national forests. But this represents less than 3 percent of the land. Should family ranching become untenable, allowing outside investors with fewer incentives to preserve the land to take over, much of the Sandhills could revert to an overgrazed, windblown state, and the ecosystem could collapse.

The stakes are high. Of the three North American prairie types—tallgrass, mixed-grass, and shortgrass—tallgrass prairie is the most endangered. In Illinois, Iowa, Indiana, Minnesota, Wisconsin, North Dakota, and Missouri, less than 1 percent of the original tallgrass prairie remains. The prairie remnants in these states, patches of grass along railway rights-of-way or in small preserves, are not large enough to support natural biological processes. The situation is similar in eastern Nebraska, where the largest remaining tallgrass preserves encompass only a few hundred acres.

One relatively large area of tallgrass prairie remains, in the Flint Hills of eastern Kansas and the Osage Hills of eastern Oklahoma. This prairie is breathtaking, with close to 4 million acres of rippling, head-high grasses. Like the Nebraska Sandhills, the region remains almost entirely under private ownership. But a good portion of the land has been reseeded with nonnative grass, and several interstate highways and turnpikes crisscross the region.

As much as 50 percent of original mixed-grass and shortgrass prairies still remain in rangeland. However, much of this rangeland has been grazed to the roots or scarred by cultivation. The largest mixed-prairie preserves lie in Badlands and Wind Cave National Parks in South Dakota and Theodore Roosevelt National Park in North Dakota. Each of these national parks encompasses between one hundred and four hundred square miles, an area sufficient to contain most native prairie species but not large enough to support genetically diverse populations of bison, elk, prairie wolves, and other large mammals. Extensive areas of mixed-grass and shortgrass prairie are managed as national grasslands—checkerboard arrangements of public and private grazing land interspersed with farmland. In most national grasslands you can't walk more than a mile or two without running into a plowed field or heavily grazed pasture.

The Nebraska Sandhills prairie—a unique composite of grasses found in tallgrass and mixed-grass prairies—covers an area comparable to all the remaining tallgrass and mixed-grass prairie preserves (national parks and national grasslands) put together. Very little of the Sandhills was ever plowed, so there is a continuity here with the past, a feeling of timelessness that is missing in most other remnant grasslands. The Sandhills may offer our best chance to preserve a sweep of prairie, a place where the grassy hills extend beyond the limits of vision.

Some people question the importance of preserving naturally functioning ecosystems such as the prairie. The response from environmentalists is too often the utilitarian, almost apologetic, "We need to preserve these natural systems because they contain plants and animals we now depend on or may depend on in the future." This is a little like saying we should preserve the Sistine Chapel because we might find some use for the ceiling plaster.

We are part of the prairie; it is part of us. We inhale moisture given off by transpiring grasses and breathe the oxygen they create during photosynthesis. We eat the seeds of wheat, barley, and rye, and the roots of other prairie plants. Our blood flows with the same molecules that nourish the big bluestem and cottonwood. Our collective memories radiate from the dusty savannas of central Africa and converge on the blood-soaked plains of the American West.

So much is already gone. The herds of 20 to 60 million bison that rolled across the landscape like restless shadows. The grizzly bears, prairie wolves, elk, and bighorn sheep. The wild, flowing flocks of curlews and upland sandpipers.

Should we destroy what remains, we will lose much more than Indian grass, black-footed ferrets, burrowing owls, and grasshopper sparrows. We will lose an irreplaceable work of creation, a critical strand in the web of life that binds us to this planet and keeps our humanity and spirit whole. We may, in Sweet Medicine's words, "become worse than crazy."

THE SANDHILLS prairie is young, but it won't remain forever. All ecosystems on earth transform over time. How will this evolution occur here? Will human indifference allow alien species to mix with the natives until the Sandhills prairie loses its identity? Will global climate change caused by pollution of the atmosphere turn the grassland to desert? Or will more natural processes act slowly on this unique prairie, enabling it to evolve into something equally wondrous?

A walk along the south rim of the Niobrara River canyon or over the uplands south of Pine Creek provides perspective. In these places you can find a precious commodity, by prairie standards. Shade. It's provided by small groves of ponderosa pines, virtually the easternmost representatives of their species in North America. These woodlands have been around for a while (homesteaders named Pine Creek during the early 1880s), but the groves are expanding.

University of Nebraska biologists Ernest Steinauer and Thomas Bragg studied the ponderosa pine woodlands growing near the confluence of Fairfield Creek and the Niobrara, thirty miles east of Valentine. By coring out individual trees and counting growth rings, they determined that 98 percent of the ponderosas became established after 1900. The oldest trees, a few dating back as far as 1870, grow in moist, north-facing canyons above the river. Groves farther south of the river consist of young trees surrounded by grassland.

Suppression of natural fires appears to have given these ponderosas a chance to compete with the dominant grasses. Lightning-caused fires, which formerly swept across the Sandhills prairie every few years, killed ponderosa seedlings without killing the deep-rooted grasses. In addition, intensive grazing by cattle has created bare patches where ponderosa seeds can take root.

The competition between trees and grasses has been going on throughout North America for millions of years, an ebb and flow driven by climatic change and the evolution of new species. Only recently have humans become major participants in this dance. Nomads who burned the grass to herd game animals contributed to the spread of prairie and the retreat of forest. Twentieth-century ranchers, who learned that controlling fire was a prerequisite to living in permanent dwellings, reversed this process. In the Missouri and Mississippi Valleys the ragged line where remaining deciduous forests yield to tallgrass prairie has migrated a couple of hundred miles westward since white settlement.

To those who have experienced the cathedral-like ponderosa pine forests of the Sierra Nevada, the trees growing above the south rim of the Niobrara River canyon may seem like pathetic imitations. The largest measure less than two feet in diameter. The brown, scaly bark on their trunks bears little resemblance to the thick, jigsaw-patterned bark of old-growth trees in California and Arizona. But to stroll among these pines is to walk on the cusp of creation. The accompanying rush of exhilaration brings the pines and the surrounding landscape into sharper focus.

Above me the olive green ponderosa canopy frames a blustery spring sky, where a pale half-moon rides through wisps of racing cloud. At my feet thousands of plump cones, reddish bronze in the morning light, rest on a bed of pine needles and green grass. I pick one up and admire the perfect symmetry, the sharpness of the silver-tipped scales, the resinous smell, and the delicacy of the papery sheaths that hold the nutlike seeds. Each little package contains all the genetic information and initial energy needed to create an entire tree. Only one seed in ten thousand will fulfill its life mission. The amount of solar energy required to push this forest a few yards farther into the prairie could provide all the power needs of a small community for years.

High in the tallest ponderosa, where a porcupine has stripped the bark from a narrow branch, a chipping sparrow trills his monotonic song. His territorial singing is fueled mostly by insects and seeds of a different kind, those of red sumac, the many-colored wildflowers growing in forest openings, and the little bluestem grass crowding the base of the trees. He and his mate will build their nest on a pine bough with a spectacular view of the grasslands, a chipping sparrow–free zone extending for miles to the north and south.

A flock of red crossbills chatter in the crown of a flat-topped ponderosa as they dismember the cones, sending a squall of scales swirling in the wind. These seed eaters wander throughout North American coniferous forests seeking out bountiful cone crops. When they find a concentration of seeds sufficient to nourish young, they stop and nest, be it June or January. Somehow these crossbills have made their way to this strip of forest, though getting here required flying over miles of prairie.

Behind me a northern saw-whet owl sits on her nest in a woodpecker hole, and a red-breasted nuthatch hammers away on a bare limb. Only fifty yards in front of me, curlews wail and grasshopper sparrows buzz in waist-high grasses.

What will this area become in a thousand years—forest, grassland, or sand desert? Our brief lifetimes condemn us to take part in this drama without ever knowing its outcome. But all our actions influence the result, just as ripples far out at sea change the height and direction of crashing waves.

I play my part, flavoring my dinner pot with pine nuts extracted from the bristly cones, pungent blond morels collected among the cottonwoods bordering the river, and a giant white puffball plucked from the swaying grasses at the forest edge.

BLUE WATER

BLUE CREEK carves its own universe from the chaos of chop hills south of Crescent Lake. Fed by dozens of artesian springs, the creek flows clear and cold through a narrow, winding valley. Brown trout and minnows dart from the cover of overhanging banks lush with green sedge and yellow coreopsis. Wood ducks and an occasional river otter raft in the strong, steady current.

Like a mountain stream misplaced in an arid landscape, the "Blue Water" maintains its strong flow during even the driest months as it navigates the forty miles from its headwaters to its confluence with the North Platte. In late summer, when the air hums with heat and the grasses turn brittle, you can still launch a canoe in this fifteen-foot-wide stream a few miles below Crescent Lake and float down to the Platte in less than a day.

Five miles north of the confluence, the Blue Water valley opens out onto the broad floodplain of the Platte. With more room to roam, the creek carves lazy oxbows while meandering through sloughgrass meadows and groves of gnarled ancient willows. Here the grasses retain their greenness well into fall, and the sweet songs of meadowlarks, orioles, and yellow warblers blend with the cries of prairie falcons and red-tailed hawks that glide out from the chalk bluffs to the west. Centuries-old tipi rings and wagon ruts scar the tablelands above the creek, and shards of flint and chert lie scattered in the grass.

It was in this opening, among the willow-lined oxbows and broken cliffs, that Little Thunder and his party of Sicangu and Oglala Lakota camped during late summer 1855. The Sicangu and Oglala were the southernmost of the seven tribes that made up the Lakota, or Teton Sioux. For decades the Lakota had lived among the deciduous woodlands and grasslands of the upper Mississippi Valley. As European American settlers pushed westward, the Lakota spilled out onto the plains, where they quickly appropriated lands occupied by the Crow, Cheyenne, and Kiowa. By the early nineteenth century the Lakota controlled an area stretching from the northern Missouri River Valley to the Bighorn Mountains of present-day Wyoming and extending south to the North Platte River.

Many Lakota revered the Sandhills as a particularly sacred place that teemed with wildlife and spirit energy. Every aspect of Lakota life emanated from a close connection with nature. In Lakota tradition the human and animal, the material and natural, flow together like wind and grass.

One Sicangu creation story tells how the Great Spirit, Wakan Tanka, grew angry with the people and unleashed a cataclysmic flood upon the earth. The people climbed to the highest hills but could not escape the rising tide. As they died, their blood congealed into a great pool.

Only one Lakota, a beautiful young woman, remained alive. She was struggling in the swirling waters when a big spotted eagle swooped down and grabbed her in his talons. He took her to a tree atop the highest of the Black Hills, the only remaining island of land. The eagle and the maiden mated, and their descendants became the Lakota nation, a people proud of their origins and their connection with the eagle, the strongest and wisest of birds.

The blood in the great pool hardened into the red pipestone used to make the *chanupah*, or sacred pipe. Thus whenever people smoke the sacred pipe, they hold in their hands the blood of their ancestors. The smoke they exhale is their ancestors' breath. That breath mingles with the essence of all life, creating a perfect union.

By the time white settlers began to creep westward along the Oregon Trail, the Lakota claimed the Black Hills and plains to the south as sacred lands given to them by the Great Spirit. Many Oglala and Sicangu considered the emigrants barbarians and tolerated their incursions into Lakota territory only so long as they brought guns, tobacco, and other gifts of industrial society. Most whites expressed similar disdain for the combative Sioux and would have been content had all their population succumbed to the cholera, smallpox, and the other imported diseases that had ravaged Sioux villages during the time of first contact with European Americans. So from the 1840s to the mid-1850s an uneasy truce, punctuated by occasional raids and skirmishes, prevailed in the Platte River Valley.

This truce unraveled in late summer 1854 when a dispute over a Mormon cow escalated into war. A group of Sicangu, Oglala, and Miniconjou Lakota had camped near Fort Laramie to receive the presents due them in return for allowing emigrants to pass through their territory. When a Miniconjou man killed a cow that had wandered into camp, the animal's Mormon owner demanded retribution. The Lakota leaders offered two horses, then five, but the cow's owner would accept nothing less than the miscreant's arrest.

Finally the fort's commander, Lieutenant Fleming, dispatched his hotheaded second lieutenant J. L. Grattan and twenty-nine men to the Indian encampment to arrest the man. As the two sides traded threats and insults, the inexperienced soldiers began shooting. All were killed by the well-armed Lakota warriors, who scalped and mutilated the bodies before leaving them to rot on the prairie.

The following summer the new agent at Fort Laramie, Major Thomas Twiss, came up with a plan to punish the Indians. He sent out word to all "friendly" tribes to move to the south side of the North Platte River, where they could receive their presents. Any Indians camped north of the river would be considered "hostile" and dealt with accordingly.

General W. S. "Whitebeard" Harney led the punitive expedition that found Little Thunder's group of Sicangu and Oglala camped along Blue Creek four miles north of the Platte. Up to this time Little Thunder had earned a reputation as a peacemaker, and there was nothing secretive or aggressive about his people's movements. But he had camped north of the river, and in General Harney's mind that was decisive.

On a misty morning in early September, Harney's troops rode up the Blue Water until they saw the cluster of tipis at the base of the bluffs. Harney sent one regiment around to the northeast to block escape routes up the valley. Accounts of what happened next differ. Some say that Harney raised the white flag, others that Little Thunder came running forward signaling that he wanted to parlay. In any event, the white soldiers kept right on coming and began firing into the encampment.

The frightened Indians retreated upriver, where they

met Harney's second regiment galloping down the valley. With nowhere to flee, the survivors scattered into the ravines and bluffs on the west side of the valley. Men, women, and children huddled in hollows in the sandstone cliffs while the federal troops blasted away with their long-range rifles. Within minutes the chalky cliffs were stained bloodred, and screams of terror had given way to muffled wails and death rattles. At least eighty-six Lakota had been slaughtered.

The blood would continue to flow for thirty-five years, at Fort Kearney, Rosebud Creek, Little Big Horn, and Wounded Knee. The accumulated bitterness and prejudice would poison relations between Indians and whites for more than a hundred years. In *An Indian in White America*, Oglala activist and social worker Mark Monroe describes growing up in Alliance during the 1950s, when Indians were confined to a tent city on the south side of town and Indian children were denied the opportunity to complete high school: "From the age of eleven clear up to the age of sixteen I would see those signs that would say, 'No Indians or dogs allowed,' and I'd find myself really thinking, 'My God, I must be an animal; people are saying I'm a dog. I can't go in there because a dog can't go in there.' "

The signs have come down, but mutual suspicion, fueled by racism, incidents of interracial violence, and chronic unemployment and alcoholism on the reservations, still haunts the "border towns" of Alliance, Chadron, Rushville, Gordon, and Valentine. Today descendants of the Sicangu and

Oglala Lakota who died on the Blue Water speak of a "buckskin curtain" separating the prosperous Sandhills ranches from the impoverished reservations a few miles to the north.

WHAT SHOULD become of a place like the Blue Water battleground? In most parts of the United States they'd erect a monument and visitors' center with a couple of curio stands. But the Sandhills are no hotbed of tourism, and here the only acknowledgment of the tragedy is an unobtrusive sign down along U.S. 26. The site itself lies within several barbed-wire fences constructed more to keep cattle in than to deter wayward tourists. Except for some ranch buildings and corrals up where the Blue Water valley begins to open out, the battleground remains in a natural state. But the residents of this predominantly Anglo-Saxon agricultural kingdom have done little to honor the memories or soothe the spirits of those who died in this valley.

Jack Grey Coon Armer, a Caddo holy man, moved to Lewellen during the late 1990s to open a trading post. After twenty-three years driving a semitrailer and raising a family, Jack settled down here with his wife, Bonnie, to carve traditional Plains Indian flutes from red cedar and to pursue his passion for nature, history, and people of all persuasions. He serves with the community's volunteer fire department, organizes old-time rendezvous and black powder shoots, and teaches traditional Native American dances to the local, mostly Anglo, scout troop. A tall, robust man with long brown hair tied back in a ponytail, Jack refers to himself jokingly as the "token Indian," and his legion of friends in Lewellen and Oshkosh call him "white boy." His Two Dogs Trading Post serves as a sort of community center where people stop to drink coffee and chat.

Not coincidentally, Jack's trading post sits beside U.S. 26 not five miles from the Blue Water battleground. He has permission from local landowners to go up there from time to time to conduct healing ceremonies.

"Someone needs to do this," he says quietly. "We lost four lodges in that fight."

We stand on a flat hilltop overlooking the valley. Below us the creek winds through greening meadows. A killdeer wings by, screaming, as we scramble down toward the water.

"It's all right little fella," Jack says. "We won't bother you."

We stroll across the hillside, stopping every few feet to pick up a flake of quartz or flint. Jack kneels by an anthill and shows me how to find beads among the shiny pebbles that the ants have gathered to protect their dwelling.

Two golden eagles soar over the valley. They swoop and tumble in what looks like courtship flight, but we notice that one has a broad white stripe on its tail and white spots on its wings—a youngster playing with its mother during these first warm days of spring. While we watch the eagles, a pair of dive-bombing prairie falcons take after them, and the four raptors weave figure eights in the pastel blue sky.

"I feel happiness here," Jack says, as we walk over the hill and face the Platte. "I feel sadness over there," he says, gesturing up the Blue Water valley.

I feel more than sadness. Would I be standing here, or anywhere on the Great Plains, had not my Irish and British forebears blasted the Sioux into submission? What do we owe to the people who died here? Are regret and compassion ever enough?

I can't think of anything appropriate to do. So I dip my hand in Blue Creek, feel my fingers begin to grow numb in the icy current, and say a small prayer of thanks for the beauty of this place.

DUNE DANCERS

No part of earth is undisrupted by humankind's acts, from the sea floor to the interior of the most remote land. Only those species that thrive on our disturbance have benefitted. The rest are at least beginning to decline. Some have vanished forever.

—Chris Clarke, "Extinction and Health"

THERE'S A meadowlark singing inside my head. The sweet warbling reverberates through the empty, drowsy spaces. I wake to blackness and the smells of wet canvas and sawdust.

As the cobwebs begin to clear, I realize that the singer is perched a few inches above me, on the roof of the photographic blind. It's a perfect post from which to survey his nesting territory and spread his message: "I'm an especially fit male meadowlark. . . . I'm an especially fit male meadowlark. . . . Females come here, males stay away." The effect is like someone playing a flute inside a trash can. I never imagined one western meadowlark could take such command of a place.

Between song bursts, I hear the high whine of the wind squeezing through the cracks and joints in the plywood walls. It chills the soul and then some, this predawn April gale that has caught me underdressed and longing for spring as I hunker down in a dank, four-foot-high box on the howling prairie. Dawn cannot come too soon.

The first hint, a thin violet wash above the eastern horizon, dims the stars slightly but does not illuminate my trembling hands. With painstaking slowness, the eastern sky turns reddish and the surrounding landscape begins to take form—first the shadows of dunes and their tossing grasses; then the lake, off to the north, flecked with dark rafts of ducks and geese; finally the lek itself, a circle of trampled grass beside the blind, where a long-billed curlew stands rigid, staring me in the eye.

I hear her mate calling over the hill, "curlee, curlee, curleeeee," a mournful wail that intertwines with the wind and splinters against the insulating wall of meadowlark song. In an instant she's gone and the lek lies empty, awaiting the main event.

"Plop . . . plop." The two grouse appear to have dropped straight from the sky. They stand motionless for a few seconds. Then, as if someone has flipped the switch or replaced the batteries, they break into their clockwork dance. Stooping down and spreading their wings, they lower their heads, cock their tails, and careen across the mowed hilltop, their feet stamping out a sound like distant machine-gun fire. They complement these gyrations with an eerie popping sound, somewhere between a "whoom" and a "bloop," created by expanding and deflating their purple throat sacs. Every few minutes the two males square off beak-to-beak before squawking, leaping into the air, and stomping back to their starting places.

As the sky blazes with color, another half-dozen males join in the dance and a couple of hens stand on the periphery, assuming an air of casual indifference. Later in the spring the females will sashay out onto the dance floor, choose partners, and sneak off into the long grass to mate. Each will lay ten to fifteen speckled brown eggs in a small hollow under a shrub or in a clump of thick grass. About three weeks later, when the chicks hatch, the mothers and their young will disperse into the hills, not to return to the booming grounds until the following spring.

Some biologists say that booming prairie-chickens and grouse become so lost in their performances that a hawk can land in their midst, eat one of them, and fly off without the others' taking particular notice. Ornithologist Arthur Cleveland Bent wrote in 1928 of a pair of coyotes that dug their den in one of the hilltops favored by strutting grouse and fed their family for weeks on the distracted dancers.

The dance seems so wildly atavistic that it's hard to believe it's real. Then I remember I've seen something like it before while watching Lakota "grass dancers." In *My Indian Boyhood*, Lakota chief Luther Standing Bear writes that birds invented dancing and that no human dancing is as orderly as that of prairie-chickens. "Their time is so perfect that even if it were performed in silence, it would be wonderful to look at. But the marvelous thing is that every bird makes a sound in his throat that is something like the double beat of a tom-tom."

Women of the Lakota Prairie Chicken Dance Association also imitated the movements of prairie-chickens and grouse, hoping to absorb some of the birds' power. As the dancers connected with the spirit of the birds, that spirit infused the dancers and the surrounding countryside with magic.

Peering out from my blind, I experience a similar transformation. The timeless, ritualized gyrations of the grouse make everything around them seem ancient and alive. I feel the dunes rising and falling, hear voices in the keening wind. My body sways to these rhythms as the birds circle, stomp, and flutter.

The sun comes up, flooding the hills with amber light. In a whir of wings the grouse vanish, and I'm left alone with the meadowlark and the wind. I crawl out of the blind, stretch, and pirouette across the lek, confident that the only beings watching are a love-crazed songbird, a distant herd of mule deer, and a sky full of spirits.

ON THESE raw April mornings, biologists at Crescent Lake National Wildlife Refuge drive the back roads at dawn to count the number of sharp-tailed grouse dancing on thirty to fifty leks, including the one where the photographic blind is erected each spring. Most leks are easy to find, since they're on hilltops, where relatively sparse grass cover gives strutting birds a view of approaching predators. During the 1990s the number of grouse seen dancing at the refuge dropped by 50 percent. No one knows the reason for this decline.

The history of sharp-tailed grouse and prairie-chickens mirrors the history of the West. These birds once strutted by the millions over the boundless tallgrass and mixed-grass prairies. Early explorers reported seeing as many as 30,000 prairie-chickens in a single flock. White hunters found grouse and prairie-chickens easy game. An August 1863 article in the Sioux City, Iowa, *Register* boasted that thirty-six men had killed 1,269 prairie-chickens in one day. The writer added, "Never . . . have prairie-chickens been as numerous as the present season." Within thirty years prairie-chickens had been driven nearly to extinction, and sharp-tailed grouse populations had been decimated.

When conservation efforts finally kicked in early in this century, much of the original prairie had been destroyed. Greater prairie-chickens, which had flourished where acorn-rich oak forests met the seed-rich tallgrass prairie, became endangered when this habitat succumbed to the plow. Lesser prairie-chickens, once abundant in the mixed-grass prairies of the southern plains, were almost wiped out by market hunters during the 1880s and again by the Dust Bowl drought of the 1930s.

Efforts to reintroduce greater prairie-chickens into the western Sandhills have failed. Competition with grouse and pheasants, along with limited availability of seeds in this most arid region of the Sandhills, may keep them from thriving. But they have expanded their range and populations slightly in southeastern Nebraska and northeastern Colorado, where remnant prairies mingle with cultivated grains.

Sharp-tailed grouse, which resemble greater prairie-chickens both in appearance and in ritual, have fared slightly better. Their historic range, extending from Alaska to Ontario, Illinois, northern Texas, and California, includes the mostly unplowed and sparsely populated Sandhills and the remote prairies and woodlands of central and northwestern Canada.

Nevertheless, these grouse have disappeared from California, most of Nevada, New Mexico, Oklahoma, and much of the Mississippi River Valley; and they are considered threatened in Colorado, Utah, and Oregon. Their recent decline at Crescent Lake National Wildlife Refuge reflects a trend observed throughout the Sandhills, despite a decade of above-average precipitation and a decrease in hunting pressure. "We hope it's just a cyclical trend," says refuge manager Bill Behrends.

Cyclical factors such as inclement weather during the nesting season, harsh winters, a short-term increase in predator populations, shortages of food (mostly seeds, fruits, and insects), or episodes of disease could affect grouse populations. However, after ten years of apparent population decline it's natural to suspect long-term changes in the grouse's Sandhills prairie environment.

The health of sharp-tailed grouse and prairie-chicken populations may reflect the health of the prairie. Some ecologists consider these birds "indicator species." These habitat specialists react with heightened sensitivity to disruption of natural processes. They "indicate" when something is drastically wrong, often long before scientists notice the disturbance.

For years, efforts to save rare and declining birds have focused on protecting remaining nesting habitat, since nest productivity is essential to species survival and nesting individuals are often most sensitive to disturbances. But in many instances where nesting habitat has been protected, species populations have continued to decline.

In Illinois, greater prairie-chickens once numbered in the hundreds of thousands, perhaps millions, nesting in tallgrass prairies throughout the state. By 1962 only about three thousand acres of native prairie remained, and the state's prairie-chicken population had declined to about two thousand individuals. Conservationists worked to protect and expand remaining nesting habitat. For a decade, the statewide population slowly increased. Then the prairie-chickens began to disappear again. By 1994 only about fifty birds remained in two isolated colonies.

Ecologists attributed the decline to nest failures. They found that the Illinois prairie-chickens were hatching fewer eggs each year and fledging fewer chicks. During some years, only 10 percent of eggs hatched. The scientists concluded that a lack of genetic variation among isolated populations was leading to a decline in genetic "fitness," dooming these populations to eventual extirpation. When researchers began to introduce prairie-chickens captured in adjacent states into the remaining Illinois flocks, nesting success increased dramatically.

Many studies have shown that as islands of protected habitat grow smaller, an array of competitors and predators can threaten native wildlife populations. Predators of prairie-chickens and sharp-tailed grouse include coyotes, red foxes, red-tailed hawks (known as "chicken hawks"), and great horned owls. Ring-necked pheasants introduced to North America from Eurasia dump their eggs in prairie-chicken nests. All these species are habitat generalists that thrive in disturbed ecosystems. As islands of native habitat become smaller and more isolated, these generalists crowd in on native species, disrupting the natural predator-prey balance that has evolved over thousands of years.

In the Sandhills, great horned owls, historically uncommon in the nearly treeless landscape, now appear to outnumber burrowing owls, which were once abundant in prairie-dog colonies. The elimination of wolves and other large predators has made life easier for coyotes. Red-tailed hawks have followed settlers and the trees they planted onto the prairie. Has increased predation by habitat generalists contributed to the recent decline in Sandhills sharp-tailed grouse populations?

It's too early to say, but even in this least fragmented of North American prairies, where thousands of square miles of native grassland remain, the signs of ecosystem disturbance and invasion by habitat generalists are hard to miss: cornfields where flocks of crows gather to feed, hay meadows full of blackbirds, raccoons draped over the branches of Russian olive trees, white-tailed deer prancing through introduced woodlands, red-tailed hawks circling over isolated homesteads.

Within this environment and the more fragmented grasslands of the surrounding Great Plains, sharp-tailed grouse and prairie-chickens are holdouts, symbols of wildness and natural well-being. They remind us how the world once looked and how it should remain.

AS GRACEFUL dancers, emblems of the windswept dunes, and indicators of ecosystem quality, sharp-tailed grouse and prairie-chickens certainly seem worth preserving. But there is something more, something that tugs at the gut, a sense that these birds are physically connected to us.

I can't watch dancing grouse without reliving those terrifying teenage gatherings when my friends and I would cower against the back wall while the coolest guys made off with the prettiest girls. The instinctive movements of courting grouse create a startling caricature of human mores. Our paths of evolution and behavior run closer than we might imagine or wish.

The Plains Indians recognized this affinity of species when they openly imitated the grouse mating dance. They sometimes called grouse and prairie-chickens "little people." In these birds they saw a level of gregariousness, mischievousness, and naïveté that reminded them of human nature.

One Lakota story tells of a wintry day when Rabbit went out hunting. He found a group of grouse maidens huddled under their speckled gray blankets on a wind-buffeted hillside. "Come here," he said. "I have a wonderful magic sack that will keep you warm." At first none of the maidens would enter Rabbit's skin bag. "We're afraid," they said.

"I'll tell you what," said Rabbit. "If you all come together, you needn't be afraid." So all the grouse gathered close together and scurried into the sack.

When Rabbit got home, he called out to his grandmother. "Look at all the fine grouse I've caught. You watch over them while I go whittle some spits to roast them with."

After a while grandmother heard tiny voices calling out from the sack. "Grandmother, let us out. We are your dear grandchildren." She asked them how they came to be in the sack. "Oh, our cousin played a joke on us," they said.

So grandmother opened the sack and the grouse flew out through the opening in the top of the lodge. "Oh, my," said grandmother, and she reached up and grabbed the last one by both legs. When Rabbit finally returned home, grandmother called out, "They all escaped, but I caught two." Rabbit could not help laughing. "Grandmother, you have only one grouse," he said, "and it has about as much flesh on its bones as I have on my paws." Off in the distance, Rabbit could hear the rest of the grouse clucking and chuckling as they fluttered across the prairie.

Those clucking sounds are becoming so rare on the Great Plains that my vivid mental images of dancing sharp-tailed grouse and prairie-chickens sometimes seem like hallucinations. This morning, as I savor a cup of coffee and stare at the empty circle of trampled grass beside the blind, I can scarcely believe that the grouse were just here, or that they'll ever come again.

PURDUM

*It's peaceful, quiet. You're able to see the sun come up
and go down. It's a pretty good place to be.*

—Bob Cox, fourth-generation Purdum rancher

"PURDUM, NEXT 5 Exits." The big green
sign protrudes from a swath of sunflowers
where the country road from Halsey glides
down into the North Loup River Valley. A quarter mile beyond, on a gentle rise above the river, stands the fine white-
steepled church, tiny post office, one-story brick bank, general store, feed store, and a dozen wood-frame houses.
Purdum, the last of the Sandhills hamlets.

During the early twentieth century the Sandhills supported dozens of small, relatively remote villages like Purdum. But the automobile, the railroads, and decreasing pop-

ulation caused a consolidation of communities, isolating those on the periphery of main transportation routes.

Of Rackett all that remains is a dusty Grange hall; of Orr, a dirt landing strip. About the last known remnant of Strasberger, a hopeful community that sprouted south of Rushville during the early twentieth century, was a pair of false teeth uncovered by a farmer plowing in the vicinity. Brownlee, where fifty-five African American families home-steaded along the North Loup River between 1900 and 1915, now consists of three abandoned stores and a portable one-room schoolhouse. Kennedy, Calora, Doughboy, Raven, Bucktail—all dissolved into the grass and sand. Somehow Purdum hung on.

I stop at the church, a tall wooden Victorian-style struc-ture erected in 1908, and wander among the scattered pews and chairs in the deserted chapel. A pile of booklets stacked on a card table catches my eye. Titled *Purdum, Nebraska, Cen-tennial, 1884–1984*, the booklets describe the town's origins and give the histories of its families.

The Nebraska Sandhills must be one of the few remain-ing places in the United States where almost everyone's family tree is public knowledge. Each county and many towns have published local histories, all written in the resi-dents' own words. Much of the information in these books has been committed to local memory, so that most folks know who their neighbors' great-grandparents were and where they came from, when the first schoolhouse was built, and how much a dozen eggs cost in 1890. No one has to work at this. It's simply part of the daily vocabulary.

I take a booklet and leave $5 in the basket. Outside the main street is empty save for two older guys sitting on the porch of the store drinking Cokes. Some blackbirds and house sparrows flit around in the elms behind the church, while a calico cat saunters across the deserted bank parking lot. A pickup cruises by, idles, then rumbles off toward Halsey. It's Saturday afternoon.

Down at the river bridge two teenage boys splash and frolic under a swarm of angry cliff swallows. The birds shriek frantically as they zoom back and forth. Beneath the bridge, baby swallow heads poke out of oven-shaped nests made of dried mud. A black-crowned night heron stands in the shallows, gazing into the cloudy current. Fields of fresh green hay and waist-high corn frame the grassy river-bank.

Purdum traces its origins to 1883, only nine years after the United States government removed the Pawnee from the Loup River region. Richard Greenland, an itinerant cowboy from Pennsylvania, and George Purdum, a homesteader from Missouri, settled on Buffalo Flats, just east of the present town site. George Purdum built a two-room house from sod and from juniper logs hauled up out of the Dismal River canyon. He, his wife, Sarah, and their three young children subsisted largely on wild game, including pronghorn shot from the front porch and ducks hunted at the area's numerous lakes and marshes.

George wrote to the U.S. Post Office Department asking for a branch in Buffalo Flats, since the nearest operating one was eighty-five miles away in Ord. The government approved his request on condition that he serve as postmaster. A community called Buffalo Flats already existed in northern Nebraska, so the new post office became known as Purdum.

Every two weeks when the mail was sent up from Ord, cowboys rode in from miles around. Sarah cooked pies and stew, and the visitors laid out their bedrolls in the house, the barn, and the nearest haystacks. When the mail finally came, usually late, George dumped it out on the kitchen table and they all helped themselves.

Historical photos of Purdum look a lot like contemporary photos. A 1910 version shows the church, a wood-frame general store, and an adjacent garage and blacksmith shop. Not far away sat a small hotel, the post office, the one-room school, and a number of houses. The bank opened in 1914.

Purdum was a tightly knit town, with dances, outdoor movies projected onto the north wall of the church, community Thanksgiving dinners, and Fourth of July picnics. In summer folks went swimming in the river or gathered at Lloyd White's pond to fish. Each fall Raymond Walter kicked off the hunting season with a big pheasant fry in his cottonwood grove.

"We had lots of barn dances, box lunch socials, picnics. It was a real community," says Roxy Keys, age ninety-two, who has lived her entire life in the Purdum area.

Roxy, a thin, snowy-haired woman with a ready laugh and engaging smile, was born in 1900 in a sod house on her family's homestead along Goose Creek, a few miles north of Purdum. Her father, an Englishman, had come to Nebraska in 1884 to work for the Burlington Railroad. He and his two brothers settled on a small piece of land near Purdum.

"They came, and oh, were they disappointed. But they didn't have money to go back."

After his wife, a German immigrant, joined him in 1888, Roxy's father staked out his homestead along Goose Creek. When he rode to Broken Bow to file his claim, all he owned was a mule and a hoe.

"He went down there with his mule to get his money for working on the railroad. He and his mule slept in a barn for three days. It cost him 10 cents and the mule 20 cents to stay in the barn. He'd had nothing to eat for two days. And a man came along with a watermelon and asked if he'd like some. Well, I guess he ate too much, because he got sick and he never would eat watermelon again. He got his money and filed, and came back up here and started building a sod house."

Her mother's garden and her father's marksmanship kept the family in food during those first few years on the homestead. Roxy's son, Keith Keys, describes his grandfather as "an amazing shot." That's how he supported his family. There was all this game—elk, pronghorn, prairie-chickens, millions of ducks. And Grandma fed everyone who came by. She had a huge pot of potatoes she'd keep going on the stove."

Roxy remembers the sod house as being comfortable and cozy. "It was a little bit darker and cool in summer and nice and warm in the winter. We always had the windows full of flowers. It was pretty good living. We piled up a big haystack of cow chips each fall and burned them all winter."

But sometimes she would wake up in winter with the blankets frozen around her face. "Chilblains, they'd drive you crazy. Sometimes you'd be out all morning and your face would be just frozen white."

As a young girl, Roxy's responsibilities included herding the pigs, chickens, turkeys, and cattle and driving the hay mower. "I raised a lot of turkeys. I raised a hundred at a time. One of my jobs as a child was to keep the coyotes from getting them. I had to get up in the morning before you could see to go along with them. I took my rifle along to keep the coyotes away. I drove a mowing machine when I was seven years old. All the women at that time worked in the hayfields. I had quite a few wrecks, including once when the horses were spooked by an automobile, took off, and flipped over the mower with me underneath."

Roxy Keys makes life on the frontier sound like a grand adventure as we sit in her son's living room beside Goose Creek. The unspoken reality is that in those times the casualties often outnumbered the survivors.

A quick reading of *Purdum, Nebraska, Centennial* lays the cards on the table: Richard and Mary Greenland, seven children born, two survived; George and Eleanor White, eleven children born, three survived; Wes and Alice Bivens, four children lost in an 1884 diphtheria epidemic.

George Purdum moved away to Idaho in 1899, shortly after the death of his young wife and their two young twins. Richard and Mary Greenland stayed on, building a frame house on the timber claim adjacent to their original homestead. Other homesteaders moved in, from Germany, England, Iowa, Missouri, and Illinois.

Roxy married Lawrence Keys and raised three children. Her son and his wife manage the ranch along Goose Creek. Keith loves the peaceful life in the Sandhills and the tradition of strong, self-sufficient families. But he misses some of the old sense of community.

"People have changed. Dad, he always told me, when he was a young fellow, all he needed was a horse and a rope. My father was a veterinarian and a blacksmith as well, he loved to work with iron. Carpentry work, they did it all themselves. You didn't take anything for granted. . . . But you know, a lot of the things we did were neighborly, back and forth, and this is what you don't see today. . . . The community used to be a community. Today, with transportation, they go everywhere, and you might not see your neighbor for a month."

FROM THE Keys family ranch I drive up the road toward Willow Lake (named by Richard Greenland for its willow grove, now under water) and on to one of my favorite campgrounds. It's marked clearly on the map as Long Lake State Recreation Area, but only a Meriwether Lewis could find it.

Fortunately, during a previous visit I had gotten directions from a local resident. "It's easy. Cross the levee, go as far as the abandoned schoolhouse, turn left, and keep going." There were no directional signs of any kind, and I had my doubts as I bounced down a two-track lane overgrown with weeds and sunflowers. I passed uncomfortably close to a white farmhouse with a middle-aged man sitting on the porch, scattered a group of chickens, and bumped my way across a grassy hillside. After a half-mile or so, I came upon an expanse of lawn and picnic tables shaded by a grove of cottonwoods. I was alone. The next morning's sunrise set the sky on fire. Greater prairie-chickens called out from the tallgrass meadows behind the campground, and snapping turtle eggs (interspersed with raccoon tracks) lay scattered along the road like Ping-Pong balls.

On this particular Saturday I'm still the only camper. I set up the tent and settle back to watch the evening's entertainment. An eastern kingbird, resplendent in his black-and-white plumage, perches at the tip of a bare cottonwood limb. Every five minutes or so he launches himself skyward and nabs a winged grasshopper. He eats ten grasshoppers in an hour. Nearby, a young red-headed woodpecker clings to a dead branch, squawking and whimpering, until an adult flies over and stuffs a cricket down its throat. Coots mutter in the cattails, and great horned owls hoot softly as the lake surface turns from crimson to slate.

At dusk a striped skunk ambles by, stopping here and there to sniff a stump or a piece of rotting bark. Shortly after she has cleared the campground, a chorus of screams and growls explodes from a nearby thicket. It's too late to move the tent, so I bury my nose in my sleeping bag and go to sleep.

THE WATER is coming up in the eastern Sandhills. It's lapping at the road to Long Lake, drowning old buildings, and inundating hundreds of acres of corn and sorghum. Ducks and Canada geese are nesting in places they've never nested before. Cows stand ankle deep in water, wondering what's become of their favorite pastures.

If you ask the locals, many will tell you it's all on account of Merritt Reservoir, southwest of Valentine. It was after its construction a few decades ago that the groundwater began rising. But during the early 1990s the groundwater level rose throughout much of the Sandhills. At Crescent Lake, a hundred miles west of Merritt Reservoir, several inches of water frequently covers the main road. The newly constructed "handicapped accessible" fishing wharf at nearby Island Lake often is accessible only to muskrats and catfish.

In an arid environment, it's easy to think that you're in a drought during average years or that things are "normal" during years of above-average precipitation. The fact is, western Nebraska hasn't experienced an extended dry period since the mid-1970s, and that dry spell was trivial compared with the full-fledged blast-furnace droughts of the 1930s and 1950s. With center-pivot irrigation on the wane in the Sandhills, there's no reason the groundwater level shouldn't be rising. Still, this reality can be confusing to folks who read that the High Plains, or Ogallala, aquifer is drying up.

In Purdum and the surrounding Sandhills, sound land stewardship and an abundance of flowing water have softened the impact of previous droughts. During the Dust Bowl years of the 1930s, when millions of tons of Great Plains soil blew away and the region's farm income declined by more than 60 percent, cattle production actually increased slightly in the Sandhills. Depressed prices for agricultural products forced local residents to get by with less, but most family ranches remained in business. So when the next drought hits, Purdum's ranching-based economy may survive while irrigated farms in more arid regions fail.

One evening several long-term Purdum residents sit around the kitchen table at Lois Gibson's lovely two-story farmhouse and answer my questions about their community's past and future. The changes they note in their lives seem minuscule compared with what most North Americans experience. The price of land is being pushed up a little by outside investors, the quality of the range is improving, the area's population is diminishing somewhat, there are fewer community activities. But the landscape and the town look and function much as they did fifty years ago.

"In ranching I'm seeing a lot more crossbreeding," says Bob Cox, great-grandson of one of the region's first homesteaders, "and we've managed the range to where it can support a lot more cattle. I think there's more grass. . . . So you're raising a lot more beef on the same acreage."

"A lot of the young people are moving on because there isn't enough land to support them," says Adah Neubauer, a third-generation Purdum resident and retired schoolteacher. "There are a number of young people who want to buy land but can't afford to do it. With the price of land, it would be pretty tough to come in and make a living. I'd be scared to death."

But everyone agrees that Purdum is still a wonderful place to live and that the town is in no danger of going under.

"I like everything," says Adah. "The fresh air and the freedom that we have, and, so far, the lack of crime. . . . You can go around with your doors unlocked and leave your keys in the car. You just don't live in fear all the time like you do in other places."

When I ask what Purdum will be like fifty years from now, everyone agrees that my question is an interesting one, but no one can frame an image of the future. "I can't think of anything right now," says Bob. "I imagine things will stay pretty much the same."

EAST MEETS WEST

They found Niobrara River to be an ideal place as they found everything they wanted to eat there, in the water, under the ground. They found wild beans and potatoes and fruits of all kinds. . . . The Niobrara [was] their home for so long they knew no other.

—Peter LeClaire, Ponca Indian historian

THE NIOBRARA River always catches me by surprise. The dirt road north from Elsmere passes through miles of Sandhills sameness: faceless hills, herds of Angus and Hereford cattle, a smattering of lakes and marshes, and a farmhouse every three or four miles. Suddenly the road plunges through ocher cliffs and pine-oak forest, and I see the stream of liquid silver winding its way eastward down the narrow valley. The view is like a scene from one of those sepia-toned wine commercials. A perfect valley, a crystalline river, surrounded by emptiness.

I park above the river and follow a trail into a forested side canyon. Ovenbirds chant from the leafy branches of white-barked birches. A white-tailed doe and her spotted fawn stand, tails twitching, in the shade of a stately oak. Deerflies cling with suicidal tenacity to my sweat-drenched neck. As I wade the icy waters of the spring-fed creek, my boots sink ankle deep into a primordial ooze of black earth, moss, and rotting stumps.

I could just as well be in Minnesota or southern Ohio. The High Plains aquifer, along with its Nahu'rac animal clan of white-tailed deer, beaver, river otters, bald eagles, kingfishers, great blue herons, and wild turkeys, has performed another miracle, creating this exotic oasis in the midst of the arid plains.

Were I more tolerant of deerflies, I could walk a mile east and find another side canyon with its own spring-fed creek and ovenbirds, wild sarsaparilla, and paper birches; and I could continue downstream, exploring dozens of forested side canyons, each created by these cool waters percolating through the Sandhills, dripping from the aquifer, tumbling down into the Niobrara. This verdant forest, the ovenbirds, the deerflies, and the sweat on my neck all spring from that fountain of life.

The aquifer transforms the climate as well as the landscape. At Valentine, thirty miles away, the temperature is 96 degrees with little humidity. Here in the valley, where the cold waters act as a natural swamp cooler, it's a steamy 83 degrees.

The heat and flies take a bite out of my search for nesting ovenbirds. But I hear a dozen of these drab little warblers singing their vociferous "tea-churr, tea-churr, tea-churr" as I zigzag down the trail. To a westerner the song suggests humid forests dripping with lichens and moss. Ovenbirds, named for their habit of building ground nests with oven-shaped entrances, flourish in mature deciduous forests of the eastern United States. Their numbers have declined where urbanization has destroyed or fragmented these native forests. West of the Mississippi they nest in isolated pockets of dense deciduous growth, including a few shady ravines in the Colorado Front Range and these moist canyons along the Niobrara.

The paper birches tell a similar story. To find other stands of this size, you have to go to the Black Hills of South Dakota or the boreal forests of Minnesota. These groves, with their wild sarsaparilla, Saskatoon serviceberry, and other northern plants, are thought to be Ice Age remnants nurtured by the cool springs and shady canyons. My walk among these birches transports me back 12,000 years to the time when forests covered much of the Great Plains.

The first white settlers called the Niobrara "the Running Water," after the Omaha-Ponca name Ni-obthatha-ke, meaning "spreading water river." With mostly loose sand and soft sandstones to hem it in, the river shifts aimlessly as it carves its course down the narrow canyon. Sandbars form and wash away as the river seeks the path of least resistance.

If you stand at the bottom of the Grand Canyon of the Colorado, you can gaze up at over a billion years of geologic change and millions of years of carving by wind and water.

The process of canyon shaping seems slow beyond comprehension. Measured against this time scale and the immensity of the canyon, human lives appear insignificant, if not irrelevant. When viewed from the bottom of the Niobrara Gorge, the earth seems younger and more pliant. That grassy bench above the canyon rim was the river bottom only 15,000 years ago. My chest is approximately at the level of the current when James McKay traveled upriver in 1795. The Niobrara has required no more than 12,000 years to carve out this canyon.

The complex forests of the Niobrara Valley are unique in North America. Nowhere else do the eastern deciduous forest and western coniferous forest blend so completely. Bur oaks, black walnuts, and lindens mingle with ponderosa pines and junipers. Red-eyed vireos from back east and red crossbills from out west and up north perch side by side.

The human element has an eastern component as well. Canoe concessions are scattered up and down the river. Private campgrounds offer green lawns and coin-operated showers. Flocks of soft-spoken, red-faced Nebraskans float down in canoes and inner tubes. Along the Niobrara below Valentine you don't need a map to know you're east of the hundredth meridian, the mythical line where the western frontier begins.

I RENT A tractor inner tube and put in at Berry Bridge, a few miles below the Fort Niobrara National Wildlife Refuge. It's early enough that no one else is on the river, and I have an escort of three great blue herons to lead me downstream. They flap from sandbar to sandbar, staying just ahead and squawking whenever I float too close. A kingfisher rattles out alarms as it zooms up the gorge. Red-eyed vireos, ovenbirds, and black-billed cuckoos sing from the shady deciduous forest on my right; red-breasted nuthatches and pine siskins from the sunwashed ponderosas on my left.

Every few hundred yards a waterfall plunges from the forest and splatters onto the sandstone shelves and sandbars at river's edge. I beach my craft and shower under a twenty-foot cascade. The sting of the water reminds me again of its source, the aquifer leaking out where the porous sandstones under the dunes meet the harder, impermeable Rosebud Formation a hundred feet above my head.

For a mile or two I float down on my back with my gear bobbing beside me. Purple martins and rough-winged swallows dart and dive overhead. The sun-dappled forests and enameled cliffs sail by like images in an IMAX movie.

I pull out for lunch at Brewer Bridge, eight miles downstream, surprising a trio of wild turkeys scratching in the leaf litter for acorns and insects. By now my slow pace has put me in the middle of the morning canoeing crowd. Shirtless teenagers rattle their paddles against the metal gunwales. Families with ice chests and picnic baskets smile as they glide by.

The Niobrara has become Nebraska's worst-kept secret. Long popular with serious canoeists, it received national attention during the early 1980s when the U.S. Bureau of Reclamation proposed building a 181-foot-high dam at Norden Chute, at the lower end of the thirty-mile stretch most popular with recreationists. Local property owners and environmentalists joined forces to fight the dam, urging Congress to designate the Niobrara a "national scenic river." One older resident sat down on a rock beside the river and informed the authorities that if they were going to build a dam they'd better bring him a snorkel because he "wasn't going anywhere."

After a bitter eleven-year fight with dam proponents and their allies from the Wise Use Movement, which opposes almost all government regulation of private lands, the conservationists won out. In 1991 President George Bush signed a bill conferring national scenic river status on a seventy-six-mile stretch below Valentine.

A number of local ranchers and some concessionaires opposed the designation, fearing it would compromise local control over lands bordering the river. For the most part that hasn't happened, but the publicity put the river squarely on the map, attracting visitors from all over the country. Recreational use has more than doubled. On a typical Saturday in late June, more than a thousand canoeists and tubers put in at Cornell Landing, east of Valentine.

My outfitter winces when I ask her about effects of the scenic designation. She bemoans the littering, water contamination, bureaucratic hassles, and pressures to convert her river frontage into a public way station with pit toilets and picnic tables. "It hasn't been that bad, but I'm not sure we needed it. We're doing okay, but we were doing fine before the designation."

Now there's talk of limiting how many people can float down the river each day, or even restricting the number of concessionaires. "It's still a gorgeous river and we love to share it with all the people who come here each summer, but sometimes I wonder."

Smith Falls State Park boasts all the amenities of a Catskills summer camp: hot and cold running water, "authentic" tipis with river views, manicured lawns, and a picnic shelter where a stern-voiced schoolteacher harangues a group of bored teenagers. Portable radios blare while campers in lawn chairs discuss the next day's canoeing plans.

Late that afternoon I wade across to the wilder south side of the canyon and climb to the top. I pass through 10,000 years of ecological succession in ten minutes. The treeless bench just south of the shoreline has probably been river bottom within the past decade. A little higher, the sand begins to sprout cottonwoods. Still farther up I enter a young grove of juniper and box elder, and then the older, shadier forest of bur oak, linden, paper birch, green ash, and ponderosa pine. Growing along the creek beside the paper birches are central Nebraska's only aspen groves. The trees are hybrids of an eastern species and a Rocky Mountain species that may have flourished in this region during the Ice Age.

When I break out on top, I'm back in the Sandhills, with not a tree for miles. The cool breeze dries the sweat from my face. The sky turns crimson. I should have camped up here.

Back at the state park, another party has pulled into the site next to mine. Armed with refreshments, I wander over that way. The group leader, John, is a biologist from Lincoln. We get to talking about the wonders of the Niobrara Valley, particularly its Edenic flavor.

"It's totally unique, a biological crossroads," he says. "You have paper birch and ponderosa pine, white-tailed deer and mule deer, cardinals and crossbills, and more hybrids here than anyplace else in North America. There's so much wildlife—wild turkeys, bald eagles, bobcats, river otters. This waterway serves as a travel corridor for all sorts of plants and animals working their way up from the Missouri Valley."

After dark, John and I walk up into the woods searching for an ecological equivalent of the hundredth meridian, a clear demarcation zone between East and West. We find a spot where we can sit, facing north, with mostly linden and bur oak on the right, mostly ponderosas on the left. We remain there in silence, soothed by the crickets, hypnotized by the patterns of moonlight and shadow on the forest floor. The eastern deciduous forest, home of my ancestors, seems musty and exotic; the ponderosas feel familiar and smell like vanilla.

Deep in the night, an anguished wail jolts me awake. I walk over to the river, expecting a porcupine. A beaver paddles back and forth in the dark current, slapping her tail at intervals, screaming inconsolably. Along the shore, a few fireflies flick on and off, oblivious to her cries. Someone snorts, a light comes on, and the spell is broken.

A HUNDRED and fifty miles below Valentine, the river dwindles into a few shallow channels before passively giving itself up to the Missouri. Just southwest of the confluence lies a spot on the map called Ponca. If you drive there along the gravel road that parallels the river, you will find a shady hillside cemetery surrounded by fields of corn and sorghum. The scattered headstones bear the names of Ponca chiefs and their kin. Two dozen bison graze in a rolling pasture. A quarter mile away, a two-story frame building covered with cedar shingles overlooks a tiny arena and a couple of tipis. A sign says "Ponca Community Center," but the building is closed for renovation and no one is around.

These are among the most visible vestiges of the Northern Ponca Indian Reservation, established by federal treaty in 1858 to protect the tribe from enemies to the north and south, from incursions by white settlers, and from the inevitable and unstoppable tide of progress and neglect. Twenty years earlier Chief Shoo-de-ga-cha (Smoke) had told the famous western artist George Catlin that there was no hope for his people's survival:

> He related to me with great coolness and frankness the poverty and distress of his nation—and with the method of a philosopher predicted the certain and rapid extinction of

his tribe, which he had no power to avert. . . . That his people had become foolishly fond of firewater, and had given away everything in their country to it; that it had destroyed many of his warriors, and would soon destroy the rest; that his tribe was too small and his warriors too few to go to war with the tribes around them; that they were met and killed by the Sioux on the north, by the Pawnees on the west, by the Osages and Konzas on the south, and still more alarmed from the constant advance of the pale faces—their enemies from the east—with whisky and small-pox, which already had destroyed four-fifths of his tribe, and would soon impoverish and at last destroy the remainder of them.

Like the ovenbirds and bur oaks, the Ponca came to the spring-watered bluffs of the Niobrara from the East. Members of the Southern Siouan language group and tracing their roots to the deciduous forests of the Mississippi and Ohio Valleys, the Ponca found themselves caught between cultures and crunched by the westward flow of peoples, both Indian and white.

They settled in the Niobrara Valley during the late seventeenth or early eighteenth century, building their fortified towns on bluffs overlooking the Niobrara, the Missouri, and a small creek, now known as Ponca, that flows in between. Their round mud-walled houses were decidedly eastern, as were their carefully crafted deerskin clothing and their dedication to a mostly sedentary, horticultural lifestyle.

The name Ponca has no known secondary meaning. Several southern tribes contained clans and subclans bearing the name, and the Ponca may have been a clan of the Omaha before splitting off to form their own tribe. Some southern tribes referred to the Ponca tribe as Pá-mase, or "head cutters," apparently because for a time the Ponca retained the middle Mississippi custom of severing their vanquished opponents' heads.

Like other Siouan peoples, the Ponca worshiped the stars and the seven directions. They synchronized their activities with the waxing and waning of the moon and the flow of the seasons. Each month had a name indicating its place in the annual cycle: Snow thaws moon (January), Water stands in ponds moon (February), Sore-eyes moon (March), Rains moon (April), Summer begins moon (May), Hot weather begins moon (June), Middle of summer moon (July), Corn is in silk moon (August), Moon when elk bellow (September), They store food in caches moon (October), Beginning of cold weather moon (November), Cold weather with snow moon (December).

Corn, beans, and squash were planted during the first moon of summer. When the corn was knee high, the chiefs met and planned the summer bison hunt. The Ponca roamed as far west as the Black Hills and Pikes Peak in their search for bison, elk, deer, beaver, and other game. They returned to the Niobrara in midsummer to tend and harvest their crops, then set out on a second extended hunt in the fall. Throughout the warmer months, the women scoured the countryside for wild strawberries, raspberries, Juneberries, wild plums, sand cherries, chokecherries, wild grapes, buffaloberries, ground-cherries, and elderberries. They made sugar from maple, hickory, and box elder sap, pounded acorns for flour, dug prairie turnips and Jerusalem artichokes, and collected other vegetables and herbs to be dried for the winter.

The valley was fruitful and would easily have sustained the five hundred to a thousand Ponca who lived there, but constant incursions by the Pawnee and Lakota, the disappearance of the bison, and the ravages of smallpox and other imported diseases made life untenable. Fearful of the Lakota, the Ponca agreed to stay on their 100,000-acre reservation and accept goods, annuities, and services from the government. Few of the goods ever made it to the reservation, only a fraction of the annuities was ever paid, and the promised schools were never built. By 1863 the Ponca found themselves worse off than ever.

In December of that year a party of fifteen Ponca men, women, and children returning from a visit to their Omaha relatives camped twelve miles south of the reservation. A group of soldiers attacked this peaceful party, killing three women and a little girl. One of the dead women was found with her clothes ripped off, and another had been almost decapitated with a saber. The soldiers were never punished, but the local Indian commissioner apologized and promised to increase the phantom annuities.

In 1868 federal negotiators eager to reach a settlement with warring western tribes awarded the Lakota a tract of land that included all of the Ponca reservation. Now totally vulnerable to Lakota depredations, the Ponca depended entirely on the trickle of annuities and the few crops they could raise within sight of army forts.

In 1877 the government decided to rectify the situation by forcibly removing the Ponca to "Indian Territory" in Oklahoma, a region known to Plains Indians as the "country of death." Chief Ma-chu-nah-zah (Standing Bear) described that journey in a court document:

> They took our reapers, mowers, hay-rakes, spades, ploughs, bedsteads, stoves, cupboards, everything we had on our farms, and put them in one large building. Then they put into the wagons such things as they could carry. We told them that we would rather die than leave our lands; but we could not help ourselves. They took us down. Many died on the road. Two of my children died. After we reached the new land, all my horses died. The water was very bad. All our cattle died; not one was left. I stayed until one hundred and fifty-eight of my people had died.

Standing Bear decided to bury his dead son in his homeland. He and thirty of his people walked the five hundred miles back to the Niobrara. Sick and nearly starved, they made it with the help of a handful of white settlers who contributed flour and cracked corn for the children and hay for the emaciated ponies. When Standing Bear and his followers reached northeastern Nebraska, they were arrested and thrown in jail.

By then local residents and some politicians had become outraged by the mistreatment of the Ponca. The *Omaha*

Daily Herald's assistant editor, Thomas Henry Tibbles, initiated a campaign to free Standing Bear and his compatriots. Two prominent Omaha lawyers, John L. Webster and Andrew J. Poppleton, agreed to file a writ of habeas corpus on Standing Bear's behalf. The lawyers argued that the government had no right to detain the chief and his followers, since they had broken no law. Government lawyers responded that Indians enjoyed no constitutional protection because they were not technically "people." After an impassioned speech by Standing Bear reputedly brought cheers from the courthouse audience, the judge summarily ruled in favor of the plaintiff.

A few days after the decision, the newly freed Standing Bear visited John Webster's house in Omaha. According to Tibbles's account, the old chief stooped down, laid his tomahawk on the floor, and spoke these words:

"You have gone into the court for us, and I find that wrongs can be righted there. Now I have no more use for the tomahawk. . . . I present it to you as a token of my gratitude. I want you to keep it in remembrance of this great victory you have gained. I have no further use for it. I can now seek the ways of peace."

An appeals court upheld the judge's decision, affirming for the first time that Indians were entitled to equal protection under the Constitution. Standing Bear and 150 of his followers settled on an island near the mouth of the Niobrara. Through intermarriage, social contact with the local

European Americans, and sale of individual allotments to white settlers, the Northern Ponca tribe slowly dissolved into the matrix of midwestern agricultural society. In 1961 the United States Congress voted to "terminate" the tribe. In the eyes of the government, the tribe of Chief Standing Bear no longer existed.

NORTHERN PONCA cultural director Phil Wendzillo and I stand on a hilltop overlooking the Missouri River. Down to our left a red-tailed hawk circles over a ravine choked with oaks and beaver ponds. In the distance the Chief Standing Bear Memorial Bridge climbs out of the marshlands, spans a broad stretch of river, and tops out above luminous limestone cliffs. Phil talks about the christening of the bridge in August 1998.

"The dedication was very special. It brought together people from so many different backgrounds, Indians and non-Indians, South Dakotans and Nebraskans, so many people working together for the same cause."

We walk through knee-high stands of needlegrass and little bluestem where the Ponca Cultural Center and tourist cabins are to be built. Phil points out the proposed site, down by the river, of a statue commemorating Chief Standing Bear. He talks of plans to expand the Ponca tribal museum, establish a store and visitors' center in the small town of Niobrara, and revive cultural traditions through native language instruction. The Northern Ponca are back.

The restoration movement began during the late 1970s, when it became clear that people were being deprived of their cultural identity and denied access to government services provided to other Native Americans. "In 1879 Standing Bear established in the federal courts that Indians were people," Phil says. "He fought for the dignity of being recognized as a man, when the government said, 'No, you're not a man, you're an Indian.' A hundred years later, after termination, if a Ponca went to a tribal health services office, he was turned away because he 'was not an Indian.' "

The path to reinstatement proved arduous. Tribal members had to establish that enough Northern Ponca still existed to constitute a tribe, that native customs and culture still flourished, and that termination had resulted in a marked deterioration in tribal members' socioeconomic status. With the help of lawyers and anthropologists, they presented their case to Congress. Their petition included the following words: "We are descendants of the Poncas—it flows through our blood peacefully like the Niobrara. We are entitled to be recognized like your descendants are recognized. We are one and the same."

For several months some Nebraska politicians, fearing the Northern Ponca would try to establish a new reservation, stalled the reinstatement effort. Finally, Ponca representatives agreed to wording in the restoration act that limits them to 1,500 acres of tribal lands, and the act was signed by President Bush on October 31, 1990.

In 1994 the Northern Ponca held their first powwow in sixty years. The opening procession featured Southern Ponca dancers who had come up from Oklahoma to teach their northern relatives. Two giant bonfires, one lit by the southern tribe, the other by the northern tribe, were brought together in the dance circle. While spectators munched on bison burgers and Indian tacos, a four-year-old boy dressed in full Ponca regalia pranced in the firelight exclaiming, "I'm a Ponca Indian!"

The powwows grow larger each year, attracting more than three hundred celebrants who travel from as far away as Mississippi and Hawaii. The tribal rolls now number nearly two thousand. Only about eighty-five live in the Niobrara region, and none is "full-blood," says Phil. He is partially of Russian descent, but he traces his Ponca ancestry back to the mid-nineteenth century. His mother's family lived on the old reservation until their farm was taken from them for $100 of debt during the Great Depression.

"I was born only two months before the tribe was officially terminated. So throughout most of my lifetime, there was not a Northern Ponca tribe. Now, when I can take a group of ten-year-old students and spend a day with them and teach them Ponca history, it's very important to me."

Since reinstatement, unemployment has gradually come down. One hundred tribal members now attend college.

Ponca language classes are filling up. "The language comes first, and from the language the true culture flows. I look for the tribe to grow, to move in new directions, whether it be small business or light industry. Once again Poncas can be proud to be Poncas. We hope this has given us a chance to make up for lost time."

That evening I stand by the Niobrara as a smoky blue mist settles over the water. I watch a family of wood ducks riding downstream and see the first fireflies emerging from the dewy grasses along the bank. The river flows gently by, its voice clear and soothing and tinged with sadness. Phil Wendzillo's optimistic words, based on an old saying, keep coming back to me: "In the circle of life, the trail never ends. It is only filled with new beginnings."

TRANSITIONS

My own feeling for tallgrass prairie is that of a modern man fallen in love with the face in a faded tintype. Only the frame is still real; the rest is illusion and dream.

—John Madson, *Where the Sky Began*

AFTER A few days on the Niobrara, I always yearn for wide open spaces and deserted campgrounds. But there's an important stop along the way. The roadside proclamation "See Nebraska's Largest Waterfall, 75¢" is too intriguing to pass up.

The Snake River Falls Café sits on a broad bench above a narrow canyon dotted with junipers and ponderosa pines. My car has the run of the gravel parking lot. A chocolate lab sprawls on the front porch, blocking the café entrance. I step over his semiconscious body and walk into a dimly lit entranceway.

"Anyone here?"

After a minute or two the proprietor, a tall, serious man wearing a white apron, emerges from the kitchen. Without a word, he takes my 75¢ and punches the keys. At the "brringg!" of the cash register, the lab springs to his feet and races toward me, tail swishing and toenails clattering against the floor. He licks my hand, swivels around, and away we go.

The trail to the falls cuts down through seventy feet of soft sandstone cliffs. The dog kicks up a cloud of fine yellow dust as he negotiates the tight switchbacks. I huff along behind, using his wildly flapping tail as a navigational fix. At the bottom he looks back, grinning, then plunges into the turquoise pool below the twenty-foot falls. He retrieves a floating stick, paddles back, and shakes himself, drenching me thoroughly.

Just as we are about to become fast friends, he glances up toward the café and sees three human silhouettes above the cliffs. He covers the intervening distance in seconds, greeting the new tour group with heightened enthusiasm.

Like so much of western Nebraska, the falls constitute topography in miniature. Take Yellowstone Falls and shrink them down to one-tenth scale. Add a slaphappy guide dog and a café with no customers, and you've captured the essence of this minimalist landscape. The 75¢ admission fee adds a nice touch.

A FEW MILES west of Valentine, the air begins to dry out. The traffic thins to a tolerable rate of one to two cars every five minutes.

I pull into the campground at Pine Lake and almost have a heart attack. Two dozen glistening white Winnebagos crowd the shoreline, like cattle at the trough. Having nowhere else to spend the night, I park in my usual spot and slink off into the woods.

A nice older couple comes by, and we get to talking. I ask where the mob has come from. "Family reunions," he says. "People like to get together once a year."

Jack is a third-generation Sandhills rancher, recently relocated to northeastern Colorado. His grandfather settled in the Mullen area during the 1880s. Jack talks about the discovery of the region by recreationists. "Used to be, folks from the eastern part of the state wouldn't come out here. I guess it was a little too bleak and wild for them. Now I have to get up a little earlier to have my favorite fishing holes to myself."

More distressing, he says, is the invasion of rich investors. "Ted Turner just bought 45,000 acres in Sheridan County. Says he wants to run buffalo. Probably doesn't know what he's doing. Then there's all this Canadian money coming in. If they take all the family ranches, they'll destroy the Sandhills."

The subject of absentee landowners and foreign investors often surfaces in conversations with Sandhills ranchers. Ted Turner's name comes up repeatedly. He has acquired more than 170,000 acres in the Sandhills and owns more than 1.5 million acres throughout the West. Turner raises bison on his Sandhills ranches. The Turner Family Foundation has committed hundreds of thousands of dollars to biological in-

ventories on their ranches. Biologists funded by the foundation are investigating the feasibility of reintroducing black-
footed ferrets and prairie wolves on a 700,000-acre Turner
Foundation ranch in northern New Mexico.

In an interview with the *Omaha World-Herald*, Turner said
his goal is to restore the prairie to its native condition:
"We're putting it back the way it was. . . . The Sand Hills
are very, very interesting, and I like them a lot. There is no
place on earth quite like them."

Nevertheless, many Sandhills ranchers are skeptical of
an outsider with limited local knowledge suddenly buying
up large chunks of land and trying to revolutionize ranching. "The main impact he's had is to raise our taxes," says
one long-term resident. "He overpays for the land, and then
our county assessments go up."

Family ranching is becoming more and more difficult. In
1910, when Caroline Sandoz Pifer was born, you could support a family on 2,000 acres. Now you need 5,000 or more,
assuming, of course, that you own the land free and clear. If
you have to make high mortgage payments, you might as
well file for bankruptcy before you start ranching. Only
people with cash reserves can afford to buy land. As family
ranches consolidate, young people must seek work else-
where. Towns stagnate. The population of Brewster, the
Blaine County seat, hovers at about forty-five. Empty buildings outnumber occupied ones along the dusty main street.

Declining beef consumption in the United States, competition with Latin American cattle operations, and rising

prices of feed and fuel have combined to make cattle ranching a tenuous proposition throughout the West. Wholesale
beef prices declined by about one-third, after inflation,
from the early 1980s to the late 1990s. One rancher who recently sold his property after decades of family ownership
told me: "It comes to a point where it just isn't worth it.
You work fifteen hours a day, worry the rest of the time,
fight the wind and cold, and when it's the end of the year
and you add things up, you're worse off than when you
started. We love the land, but we can't afford to stay here."

Henry Rudnick, preparing to retire after living on the
same ranch near Ainsworth for sixty-five years, was hoping
someone from the community would buy his land and continue the dairy farming operation: "There's lots of young
people who would like to get into the business," he says,
"but they can't afford to make mortgage payments. Most of
our offers are coming from outside investors. Some just
want a place for a summer home or to lease out."

It's a familiar story, a scenario created by corporate competition, an archaic system of government subsidies that fa-
vors ranchers who graze their stock on public lands, and an
absence of environmental planning. While cattle munch
away on the most marginal of habitats, including deserts in
Nevada and Utah and ravaged rain forests in Costa Rica,
much of this exquisite prairie, a landscape that evolved with
and sustained herbivores for thousands of years, could
eventually be sold out to the highest bidder and converted
to game parks and ranchettes.

Even on family-owned ranches, economic pressures sometimes motivate landowners to disrupt the natural order to increase profits. High-yield exotic grasses such as timothy, smooth brome, and orchard grass have been planted in hay meadows. These introduced species quickly take hold and spread, threatening native grass communities. A 1990 study conducted in Grant County estimated that fifty-five wetlands, comprising thousands of acres, had been drained to create hay meadows. Ranchers in Cherry County have used a system known as "ditching" to drain fens that contain rare plant communities. Ditching is no longer permitted, and the Nature Conservancy, along with an organization called the Sandhills Task Force, has forged public-private agreements to protect wetlands. Still, most ranchers continue to maintain their ditches, a practice permitted under current law.

As a solution to economic stagnation on the Great Plains, some environmentalists advocate turning large chunks of the remaining grasslands into nature preserves, where bison and pronghorn can roam free and Plains Indians can recapture their heritage. The problem with proposals of this sort is that they're often concocted by urbanites who know little about the prairie and have little appreciation for the conservation efforts of many ranchers. When Rutgers University professors Frank and Deborah Popper toured Nebraska to promote their plan for a 139,000-square-mile "buffalo commons" on the High Plains, most residents listened politely and then told the Poppers "No thanks." In *Where the Buffalo Roam*, Anne Matthews quotes the director of the Center for Great Plains Studies at the University of Nebraska: "It really should be called the Buffalo Bill Commons Wild West Show. This is a degrading proposal for Native Americans and all other Plains residents. We, in short, are the zoo."

A more modest Sandhills prairie preserve, large enough to sustain prairie wolves, bison, and elk, could become a major tourist attraction that would provide a boost to the local economy. Already, bird-watchers flocking to the South Platte to observe the sandhill crane migration inject about $15 million a year into the Grand Island economy. Niobrara River canoeists have a similar impact in Cherry County.

In *Ecology and Economics of the Great Plains*, Daniel Licht proposes creating a publicly managed 5,409-square-mile reserve in the northwestern Sandhills. The federal government would acquire most of the land for the reserve by offering to buy existing ranches at above market value. Licht estimates that bison harvests and hunting fees in a reserve of this size could generate $20 million a year, equivalent to the current net annual value of agricultural products in the region. However, he adds these words of restraint: "Of all the large ecotypes in the grassland biome, the Sandhills may be as close as any to its pre-Columbian condition. . . . Therefore establishing a Sandhills ecological reserve seems less compelling than conserving many other sites."

Regardless of how compelling the need for a preserve might be, it's hard to imagine fiercely independent Sandhills ranchers ever signing off on a plan that would result in the federal government's owning and managing 25 percent of the region. It's much more likely that continued public-private partnerships involving the U.S. Fish and Wildlife Service and conservation groups such as the Nature Conservancy will lead to an incremental restoration and preservation of Sandhills wetlands and grasslands.

With or without large nature preserves, the buffalo are coming. In addition to Ted Turner's operations, a dozen private ranches throughout the Sandhills raise bison. The Nature Conservancy's Niobrara Valley Preserve and the Fort Niobrara National Wildlife Refuge, east of Valentine, manage their own herds. The total North American bison population now exceeds 200,000, a far cry from historic numbers but a significant improvement since the late nineteenth century, when only about 1,000 remained.

The staff at Crescent Lake National Wildlife Refuge has developed a plan to create a 24,000-acre wilderness area and stock it with bison. Hunters would purchase permits to stalk the bison on foot or on horseback.

"In some ways, bison are easier to manage than cattle," says refuge manager Bill Behrends. "They don't require inoculations, and they don't need help calving." He sees bison ranching, combined with hunting, as the wave of the future. Currently, however, the high cost of fencing and of stock (bison heifers go for up to $3,000 apiece) discourages most ranchers from considering conversion from cattle to bison.

Many ecologists characterize bison as a "keystone species," a critical component of healthy Great Plains prairies. Modern bison evolved with the prairie grasses. Their grazing stimulated new growth and created room for less palatable plants. By wallowing and kicking up soil they created ephemeral wetlands and patches of bare ground where highly specialized plants could grow. By urinating and defecating they added nitrogen to the soil. Decay of dead bison also contributed to soil nitrification, and the carcasses provided food for a range of predators and scavengers, including wolves, coyotes, grizzly bears, swift foxes, vultures, eagles, and ravens.

Plains Indian life revolved around the enormous bison herds that once darkened the prairies. Every part of the bison, from the horns to the bladder, was used and considered sacred. To many descendants of the nomadic bison hunters and to many ecologists, a Great Plains grassland without bison will never qualify as a natural prairie.

Cows have replaced bison as the Sandhills prairie's dominant herbivore. To some extent they mimic the grazing patterns of bison. In fact, cows are genetically close enough to bison to produce hybrid offspring (the famous "beefalo"). But cows don't move around much. The bison herds denuded some areas of the prairie while leaving others untouched. Cows stay within the barbed-wire fences, mowing the grasses and forbs (herbs other than grass) down to a uniform length. They also tend to select different plants to graze on. Bison, and their digestive systems, evolved with the tough-stemmed, silica-rich grasses of the North American prairie. Cows, which evolved under different conditions in Eurasia and Africa, often favor the more succulent forbs.

By changing the natural plant composition of the prairie, cows influence wildlife populations as well. The grazing patterns of bison created a mosaic of short and tall grasses necessary to support the full complement of prairie birds. Under today's more uniform grazing regime, Great Plains populations of mountain plovers and lark buntings, species that thrive in close-clipped grasslands and disturbed areas, have declined. So have numbers of upland sandpipers and grasshopper sparrows, which typically nest among the taller grasses. An alarming decline in numbers of swift foxes on the western plains may also stem from the elimination of bison. Ecologists believe these small foxes may have depended on bison carcasses for a large portion of their food.

Despite the ecological arguments for replacing cows with bison, many Sandhills ranchers fear that stocking bison on fenced ranches managed by absentee owners will lead to degradation of the range. As proof, they cite incidences of overgrazing on some bison ranches. "This grassland never supported very many bison," one rancher tells me, while another laments, "Everybody's concerned about protecting endangered species; well, *we're* the real endangered species."

In a place that seems suspended in time and barely touched by the neurosis of modern society, talk of revolutionary change is scary. Along with so many Sandhills ranchers, I'd love to see the landscape stay exactly as it is now. But I know the price: a habit of constantly glancing over your shoulder, flinching at any hint of a threat to the serenity of this prairie island.

WHILE JACK and his wife go off looking for bass, I sit in the shade watching the pelicans, motorboats, and Winnebagos. A low-slung Chevy carrying four teenagers rumbles by, blaring rap music. The revelers pull into a campsite and sit on the hood, chugging beers and shouting epithets. I wonder about Roxanne, unaccounted for since last fall, and the great horned owls perched somewhere in the pines.

Thoroughly discouraged, I pack up and head out toward Crescent Lake. I stop for a late afternoon supper at one of my favorite Sandhills restaurants, a six-table café nestled beside the railroad tracks near State Highway 2. The place is deserted, and a "Closed" sign sits on the windowsill. I gaze back up toward the highway. I've seen this coming.

A few years ago, someone built a modern edifice next to State Highway 2 and christened it Stockman's Restaurant. Someone also put up a billboard urging motorists to turn off and take "the back route to the Black Hills via scenic Pine Lake." If I owned a chain saw, that billboard would have come down long ago. So I've been boycotting Stockman's and taking my business to Jerry's Café, where the food is wholesome and the owners always have time to sit down and chat about ongoing developments.

I'm starving, so I sell out. The proprietor at Stockman's greets me, her only customer, and hands me a menu. I order what appears to be the only nonbeef offering, a "chicken fry." We talk. Somehow the conversation comes around to the subject of wild turkeys. I tell her about my off-and-on relationship with Roxanne.

"That must be one of my turkeys," she says.

"Your turkeys?"

"A while back I got a permit from Game and Parks to raise wild turkeys and release them. It was pretty tricky. We had to feed them through an opening in the wall of the barn so they wouldn't imprint. Then one day they all took off and started walking north."

"North?"

"They followed the highway for a mile or so, and then we lost track of them. But reports keep coming in."

I pay for my meal, a delicious deep-fried steak, and shuffle out into the late afternoon sunlight.

Heavy equipment is hard at work on the road to Crescent Lake. Not a new highway! I might be able to live with Roxanne's being a refugee from turkey rehab and with RVs descending on Pine Lake, but not with conversion of this sublime, anachronistic, annoyingly bumpy pathway to wilder places and simpler times. I drive about sixty miles an hour, dreading what I'll find around the next bend.

The highway narrows to the requisite one and one-half lanes of oil and sand, and the heavy equipment exits the rearview mirror. Soberly, I realize that a lot of Garden

County's residents would love to see the road improved, but with the local population declining and many businesses stagnating, there's barely enough money in the county till to adequately maintain the highway, much less reconstruct it.

I stop at a curve where a steep dune towers over an expanse of marsh. I sit in the shade, take off my shoes and socks, and bury my feet in the cool sand. A flock of cormorants skim over the cattails and bulrushes. Hundreds of ducks paddle around in the shallows, whistling, cackling, grunting. Shadows course over the hills as thunder rumbles off to the west.

CRESCENT LAKE

*Earth is your Grandmother and Mother, and She is
sacred. Every step that is taken upon Her should be as
a prayer.*

—Black Elk, *The Sacred Pipe*

At Crescent Lake the setting sun illuminates the rain-freshened prairie with glow-
ing apricot light. Purple black thunder-
clouds rumble away to the east, where lingering streaks of
lightning dance across the horizon. A lone white pelican
drifts lazily on the lake's placid surface, gently rocking the
reflections of distant chalk bluffs and shadowy green hills.

There are no people about and only a few signs of
human visitation: the narrow road threading its way northward toward the wildlife refuge, a steel waterfowl observa-
tion tower gleaming in the sunlight on a far hill, and the
rusting chassis of a pickup truck abandoned incongruously

in the shallows, a few yards out from shore. The truck, a monument to continuity and permanence, has not moved in more than a decade. For now it serves as an avocet feeding area. The avocets wade daintily among the wreckage, sweeping their long, upturned beaks back and forth through the briny water like metronomes.

Except for some deterioration of the submerged truck, this lakeshore remains unchanged since my first idyllic evening in the Sandhills many years ago. As then, I'm alone with the birds, the grass, and the expansive sky.

I walk along the deserted road, where a raucous crowd of yellow-headed blackbirds flit and fuss as they jostle for perches in the cattails. A nighthawk descends from the firmament and floats by, nearly brushing my shoulder. It rises, turns, and swoops again, passing within inches of my head. I stop and stand dead still. A mosquito settles on my bare arm. The nighthawk swishes past, sending a small cloud of insects swirling in its wake.

Awesome birds, nighthawks. At night these large-headed relatives of whip-poor-wills skip across the sky, enormous mouths open, seining insects from the air much as whales strain plankton from the sea. By day they sleep contentedly on fence posts, calm as cats. I've approached to within ten feet of a sleeping nighthawk without its taking any particular notice. No wonder Plains Indian stories treat them with such wonder and respect.

A Cheyenne story tells how Wihio the trickster incurred the wrath of a great stone by asking it to turn over more than four times. The stone chased Wihio down the hillside and across the prairie. When the exhausted Wihio fell down, the great rock landed on top of him.

Wihio cried for help, but none of the animals that came by, not even the great bison, could move the stone. Finally he saw a nighthawk flying overhead and called out to it, "Hey, fart-bird, this stone has been saying bad things about you; it said you have a round head and big eyes, a pinched up beak and a wide mouth, and that you are a very ugly bird. I told him not to speak so, but when I said this to him he jumped on me and holds me down."

The nighthawk, deeply offended, flew high up into the sky and then shot straight down, striking the stone and shattering it into many pieces. Wihio walked away unharmed.

Nighthawks dive at more than sixty miles an hour. A single nighthawk can gobble up more than a million insects during its lifetime. When it comes to nesting, nighthawks are opportunistic, laying their eggs just about anywhere: in shallow depressions on sandy soil, on top of rotting stumps, in abandoned robin nests. Some even lay their eggs on gravel roofs. They rely on broken-wing acts and other distractions to deter predators.

During the mid-nineteenth century, when gravel was introduced as roofing material on flat roofs, nighthawks became common in some North American cities. However, destruction of native prairies has led to their decline in many areas. They seem to thrive in the Sandhills, where there is no shortage of grass, insects, or barren ground.

The white pelican is another Sandhills success story. During the middle of this century this inland waterbird disappeared from much of its North American nesting range. Nesting colonies, which are on predator-safe islands in the middle of large lakes or reservoirs, declined from a North American total of twenty-three around 1900 to fewer than ten by 1960. Drainage of marshes and pesticide poisoning of fish threatened the species' survival.

Since about 1970 the number of nesting colonies has begun to increase, and some colonies have become more productive than ever. Although none of the colonies lies within the Sandhills, thousands of preadolescent birds summer in the region, and some adults, which can easily cover sixty miles or more on foraging flights, visit Sandhills lakes to scoop up fish in their enormous bills. With wingspans exceeding nine feet, these buoyant flyers add grace and a sense of the exotic to the prairie landscape.

Trumpeter swans, known to the Lakota as keepers of the sacred southern path toward the sun, have returned to the Sandhills after a long absence. Few or none nested there during the first half of this century, when habitat destruction in breeding grounds throughout North America nearly drove the species to extinction. Now at least a dozen pairs glide across Sandhills lakes with their fluffy young cruising behind. A pair has even returned to Swan Lake, south of Hyannis.

Biologists reintroduced trumpeter swans to historic nesting areas in Wyoming and South Dakota, but this species and the white pelican were saved largely by protection of breeding habitat, controls on hunting, and restrictions on pesticide use. Similar measures have helped bald eagles and ospreys, which winter along Sandhills rivers and streams. Less than a mile from where I stand, a pair of bald eagles nurture their young in a bulky stick nest high in a cottonwood tree. This may be the first bald eagle nest ever noted in the western Sandhills. The Cheyenne and Lakota often spoke of the white-headed eagle, guardian of the people's health and bearer of the North Wind, but they and nineteenth-century explorers left no records or descriptions of bald eagle nests in this nearly treeless land.

Captive breeding and reintroduction programs have restored wild turkey and river otter populations. Other species have recovered without any particular attention from biologists. Mountain lion sightings are becoming more and more frequent in the pine bluffs bordering the Sandhills to the north and south. Sandhills breeding populations of American bitterns, Swainson's hawks, and northern harriers (marsh hawks) appear to be thriving, probably because most ranchers do a good job of conserving wetlands and natural grasslands. That this privately owned and managed region has become a hot spot for wildlife watching proves you don't have to invest millions in studies and recovery programs to save most species. Set aside the habitat and manage it sensibly, and most birds and mammals will return. The trouble is we're running out of habitat.

A popular wall map titled "The United States at Night" shows the pattern of lights across the country as seen from a satellite on a perfectly clear night. There are half a dozen "black holes" on the map, large areas where no lights are visible. Five of the dark areas lie in the Great Basin. Just one lies east of the Rockies. When I stand alone in that patch of tranquillity and see the pelicans and nighthawks sailing overhead, hear the frogs and cicadas chorusing, watch pronghorn and white-tailed deer racing across the hills, the conclusion is obvious: too many of us, not enough places like this.

MY NIGHTHAWK leaves me to resume his daredevil courtship flight high overhead. I can hear his persistent call, a harsh "peeant," and an occasional, fartlike "vroorrr" as he plummets toward his mate on the ground and the wind rushes through his wing feathers.

As the nighthawk dances away into the distance, a long-billed curlew comes winging toward me. Resembling a B-1 bomber on a radar-evading run, it skims across the switchgrass and prairie sand reed, homing in on its apparent target—my head. The curlew veers off at the last second, and I can still feel the prop wash as it circles and lines up for its next run. A second curlew locks into the flight pattern, followed by a third.

I hold out my arms like a scarecrow, challenging them to take their best shot. They zoom by, one on the right, another on the left, their comically large beaks bleating out frenzied warnings, their tawny feathers catching the last glint of sunlight.

Two willets, amused or encouraged by the onslaught, join in. A pair of Forster's terns appear out of nowhere and take up the attack. Birds are homing in from all directions, wheeling, diving, screaming.

I don't take the assaults personally. On the contrary, it's thrilling to be in the middle of things for a change, rather than on the outside looking in. The birds seem to be having a fine time as well. But I hate to disrupt their nesting routine. I ease my way out of the maelstrom and head back the way I came.

The sun sinks below the horizon, and the western sky dims to a steel gray. The froglike "oonk-a-loonk" of an American bittern drifts out across the marsh. A great blue heron sails over the cattails, croaking gruffly.

As the cooling air settles, the deep blue dome of sky and drifting stratus clouds form a canopy of softening light that cradles sound and quiets thought. Breaths mingle in the still air. Shadow and spirit converge in the twilight.

What begins as a barely perceptible humming grows steadily louder, becoming a high, irritating whine. I can't locate the source and imagine for a moment that the sound emanates from inside my head. Then I notice the insects, clouds of them rising up off the lake and out of the marshes, coming my way. Time to head out.

Along the Oshkosh–Lakeside road, little burrowing owls perch on the sandy shoulder where worms and insects have been flushed out by the evening rain. As the car rattles along, one owl after another flutters up into the headlights, hovers there for a moment like a giant moth, and vanishes into the night.

BIBLIOGRAPHICAL ESSAY

Introduction

The Arapaho story is adapted from Alice Marriott and Carol K. Rachlin, *American Indian Mythology* (New York: Thomas Y. Crowell, 1968), 194–95.

The presence of seashells on the arid prairie has astonished many writers. Hal Borland offers a particularly poetic description of how discovering a fossilized clamshell helped him understand the scope of time in *High, Wide, and Lonesome* (Tucson: University of Arizona Press, 1984), 232–33.

Landmarks

The epigraph on page 1 appears in Luther Standing Bear, *My Indian Boyhood* (Lincoln: University of Nebraska Press, 1988), 13. Luther Standing Bear, a Lakota chief, lived from 1868 to 1939. See also Luther Standing Bear, *Stories of the Sioux* (Lincoln: University of Nebraska Press, 1988).

Ancient Voices

For a readable, comprehensive description of the paleontology and archaeology of Nebraska, see "The Cellars of Time," *Nebraskaland Magazine* 72, no. 1 (1994), special publication.

Some scientists believe Clovis hunters caused the massive extinctions of large Ice Age mammals such as mammoths and sloths. Others believe rapid climate and vegetation change caused these extinctions. See Jared Diamond, "The American Blitzkrieg: A Mammoth Undertaking," *Discover* 8 (June 1987): 82–88; and Paul S. Martin and Richard G. Klein, eds., *Quaternary Extinctions: A Prehistoric Revolution* (Tucson: University of Arizona Press, 1984).

American Indian crane stories are recounted in Frank Hamilton Cushing, *Zuñi Folk Tales* (Tucson: University of Arizona Press, 1992), and George Bird Grinnell, *By Cheyenne Campfires* (Lincoln: University of Nebraska Press, 1971). See also Stith Thompson, *Motif-Index of Folk Literature*. 6 vols. (Bloomington: Indiana University Press, 1989).

Aldo Leopold writes about cranes in *A Sand County Almanac* (New York: Ballantine Books, 1966), 102–3.

Four Winds

The epigraph on page 16 is from Black Elk, *Black Elk Speaks: Being the Life Story of a Holy Man of the Oglala Sioux*, as told through John G. Neihardt (Lincoln: University of Nebraska Press, 1979), 194–95.

This version of part of the Lakota creation myth is adapted from William Powers, *Oglala Religion* (Lincoln: University of Nebraska Press, 1977), and James R. Walker, *Lakota Belief and Ritual* (Lincoln: University of Nebraska Press, 1980).

Black Elk describes the powers of the Four Winds in Wallace Black Elk and William S. Lyon, *Black Elk: The Sacred Ways of a Lakota* (New York: Harper San Francisco, 1990), 39. John Lame Deer's description of prairie weather appears in John Lame Deer and Richard Erdoes, *Lame Deer, Seeker of Visions* (New York: Washington Square Press, 1972), 114.

Excerpts from Maghee's 1873 diary appear in Charles Lindsay, "The Diary of Dr. Thomas G. McGee," *Nebraska History* 12, no. 4 (1929): 247–304.

Ora A. Clement writes about the "schoolchildren's storm" in Virginia Faulkner, ed., *Roundup: A Nebraska Reader* (Lincoln: University of Nebraska Press, 1957), 263–68. H. E. Clements's account appears in Sheridan County Historical Society, *"Recollections" of Sheridan County, Nebraska* (Gordon, Nebr.: Sheridan County Historical Society, 1976), 154–56.

Shifting Sands

The epigraph on page 26 is from George E. Hyde, *Life of George Bent, Written from His Letters* (Norman: University of Oklahoma Press, 1968), 155.

For a fascinating account of how scientists have measured the age of the dunes, see Ann Bleed and Charles Flowerday, eds., *An Atlas of the Sand Hills* (Lincoln: Conservation and Survey Division, University of Nebraska, 1989), 29–56, and Jon Mason, James Swinehart, and David Loope, "Holocene History of Lacustrine Sediments in a Dune-Blocked Drainage, Southwestern Sand Hills, U.S.A." *Journal of Paleontology* 17 (1997): 67–83. Gerry Steinauer describes the natural history of Sandhills fens in "Sandhills Fens," *Nebraskaland Magazine*, July 1992, 16–31.

Pawnee Springs

Chief Terrecowah (page 35) is quoted in Martha Royce Blaine, *Pawnee Passage: 1870–1875* (Norman: University of Oklahoma Press, 1990), 214.

Grinnell recounts the story of the young man who came back to life in *Pawnee, Blackfoot, and Cheyenne: History and Folklore of the Plains, from the Writings of George Bird Grinnell*, edited by Dee Brown (New York: Charles Scribner's Sons, 1961), 63–67.

Pawnee origin myths and customs are discussed in detail in Gene Weltfish, *The Lost Universe* (New York: Basic Books, 1965), and Grinnell, *Pawnee, Blackfoot, and Cheyenne*. Grinnell explains the origins of tribal names in *Pawnee Hero Stories and Folk-Tales, with Notes on the Origins, Customs, and Character of the Pawnee People*, introduction by Maurice Frink (Lincoln: University of Nebraska Press, 1961), 236–48. The story of the birth of dawn is related in George Cronyn, *American Indian Poetry* (New York: Fawcett Columbine, 1991), 237–42.

Estimates of Pawnee deaths in Massacre Canyon range from sixty-nine to more than one hundred. The account of Chief Tirawahut Resaru killing his own son comes from a Pawnee informant quoted in Martha Royce Blaine, *Pawnee Passage*, 139.

The captive girl sacrifice has been described in numerous sources, including Gene Weltfish, *The Lost Universe*, 129–43.

The story of how Mother Moon taught the Pawnee to grow corn and hunt bison appears in George Dorsey, *The Pawnee Mythology* (Lincoln: University of Nebraska Press, 1997), 21–28.

The entire text of Chief Petalesharo's speech is included in W. C. Vanderwerth, *Indian Oratory* (New York: Ballantine Books, 1971), 67–71.

For a detailed and moving account of the taking of Pawnee lands, see David Wishart, *An Unspeakable Sadness: The Dispossession of the Nebraska Indians* (Lincoln: University of Nebraska Press, 1994), 124–32, 189–201, and 240. Grinnell's comment about Pawnee removal appears in Blaine, *Pawnee Passage*, 214. Blaine quotes Lone Chief and Chief Terrecowah on 215.

Grass

Grace Snyder describes hearing the grass grow in *No Time on My Hands* (Lincoln: University of Nebraska Press, 1986), 116.

For grasshopper stories, see Joanna L. Stratton, *Pioneer Women* (New York: Simon and Schuster, 1982), 101–6, and John Ise, *Sod and Stubble* (Lincoln: University of Nebraska Press, 1968), 49–53. John Madson describes the enormous swarm that descended on Nebraska in *Where the Sky Began* (Boston: Houghton Mifflin, 1982), 163–64.

Wilber, Aughey, and Goddard are quoted in David Emmons, *Garden in the Grassland: Boomer Literature of the Central Great Plains* (Lincoln: University of Nebraska Press, 1971), 52–53, 135, and 21.

Memoirs from the Waggoner and Fairhead families appear in Sheridan County Historical Society, *"Recollections" of Sheridan County, Nebraska* (Gordon, Nebr.: Sheridan County Historical Society, 1976), 271–78. Eleanor Mc-Clung, granddaughter of Joseph Fairhead, provided additional recollections written by family members.

Nellie Bly was the pen name of Elizabeth Cochrane, who was most famous for circumnavigating the globe in less than eighty days. Her articles from western Nebraska are quoted in T. D. Nostwich, "Nellie Bly's Account of Her 1895 Visit to Drouth-Stricken Nebraska and South Dakota," *Nebraska History* 67, no. 1 (1986): 30–67. For a fascinating account of the social impact of the 1890s agricultural disasters, see Marshall Bowen, "Environmental Perception and Geographic Change in Southwest Sheridan County," *Nebraska History* 51, no. 3 (1970): 319–38.

Pine Lake

For riveting accounts of the habits and decline of the long-billed curlew, see Peter Matthiessen, *The Wind Birds* (New York: Viking, 1981), and Arthur Cleveland Bent, *Life Histories of North American Shore Birds*, part 1 (New York: Dover, 1962).

Melvin Gilmore writes about spiderwort in *Uses of Plants by the Indians of the Missouri River Region* (Lincoln: University of Nebraska Press, 1977).

Tallgrass Desert

The Ian Frazier epigraph on page 77 is from *The Great Plains* (New York: Farrar, Straus & Giroux, 1989), 157.

McKay's account is quoted in Aubrey Diller, "James McKay's Journey in Nebraska in 1796," *Nebraska History* 36, no. 2 (1955): 127. Warren's journey is described by Vincent Flanagan in "Governeur Kemble Warren, Explorer of the Nebraska Territory," *Nebraska History* 51, no. 2 (1970): 186. Hayden's account is quoted in Lloyd McFarling, *Exploring the Northern Plains, 1804–1876* (Caldwell, Idaho: Caxton, 1955), 223.

Tree-ring data and more detailed nineteenth-century descriptions of blowing and drifting sand appear in Daniel Muhs and Vance Holliday, "Evidence of Active Dune Sand on the Great Plains in the Nineteenth

Century from Accounts of Early Explorers," *Quaternary Research* 43 (1995): 198–208.

D. L. Bliss writes of his years as a Sandhills rancher in *Panhandle Vale, Sandhills Trail: Reminiscences of a Nebraska Rancher* (New York: Exposition Press, 1960).

Thomas B. Bragg summarizes the role of fire in "Fire History of a North American Sandhills Prairie," *Program of the Fourth International Congress of Ecology* (Syracuse: State University of New York, 1986). James Stubbendieck discusses Sandhills range conditions in Ann Bleed and Charles Flowerday, eds., *An Atlas of the Sand Hills* (Lincoln: Conservation and Survey Division, University of Nebraska, 1989), 227–31.

James C. Dahlman's account of the discovery of the Sandhills cattle range appears in Marianne B. Beel, *A Sandhill Century: A History of Cherry County, Nebraska*, 2 vols. (Valentine, Nebr.: Cherry County Centennial Committee, 1986), 1:12. See also J. C. Dahlman, "Recollections of Cowboy Life in Western Nebraska," Nebraska History 10, no. 4 (1927): 335–39.

The murder of Emile Sandoz is described in Mari Sandoz, *Old Jules* (Lincoln: University of Nebraska Press, 1935), 307–26. The murder of O. F. Hamilton has been meticulously reconstructed by Nellie Snyder Yost in "Nebraska Skulduggery and the Origin of the FBI," *American West*, August 1988, 58–62.

Crites's statement is quoted in Bartlett Richards Jr. and Ruth Van Ackeren, *Bartlett Richards, Nebraska Sandhills Cattleman* (Lincoln: Nebraska State Historical Society, 1980), 170. For Richards's letters, see 158 and 197–219.

Whitetails

The story of the deer woman who seduces the young man and drives him crazy (page 90) appears in various sources, including John J. Powell, *Sweet Medicine: The Continuing Role of the Sacred Arrows and the Sacred Buffalo Hat in Northern Cheyenne History*, vol. 2 (Norman: University of Oklahoma Press, 1969), and Karl Schlesier, *The Wolves of Heaven: Cheyenne Shamanism, Ceremonies and Prehistoric Origins* (Norman: University of Oklahoma Press, 1987).

Francis Parkman describes the Platte River Valley in *The Oregon Trail* (Garden City, N.Y.: Doubleday, 1946).

The effects of white-tailed deer on North American forests are summarized by Stephen B. Jones, David DeCalesta, and Shelby E. Chunko, "Whitetails Are Changing Our Woodlands," *American Forests*,

November–December 1993, 20–25. Rory Putnam discusses deer behavior in *The Natural History of Deer* (Ithaca, N.Y.: Comstock, 1988).

John Lame Deer talks about deer's second sight and invincibility in John Lame Deer and Richard Erdoes, *Lame Deer, Seeker of Visions* (New York: Washington Square Press, 1972), 125.

The Ponca story appears in Alice Marriott and Carol K. Rachlin, *American Indian Mythology* (New York: Thomas Y. Crowell, 1968), 161–64; the Pawnee story is in George A. Dorsey, *The Pawnee Mythology* (Lincoln: University of Nebraska Press, 1997), 380–81. This version of the story about the deer that adopted the sun child is adapted from Frank Hamilton Cushing, *Zuñi Folk Tales* (Tucson: University of Arizona Press, 1992), 132–50.

A Sense of Home

Mari Sandoz wrote of her time in Lincoln and her relationship with her father in her autobiographical notes, published in Caroline Sandoz Pifer, *Making of an Author: Mari Sandoz, 1929–1930* (Crawford, Nebr.: Cottonwood Press, 1982), 11–13 and 70. See also Caroline Sandoz Pifer and Jules Sandoz Jr., *Son of Old Jules* (Lincoln: University of Nebraska Press, 1987). *Old Jules* (Lincoln: University of Nebraska Press, 1935) and Helen Winter Stauffer's *Mari Sandoz, Story Catcher of the Plains* (Lincoln: University of Nebraska Press, 1988) probably offer the most accurate and comprehensive picture of her life.

Caroline Pifer no longer maintains the museum, but she still sells books and welcomes visitors at her ranch house south of Gordon.

Lost Chokecherry Valley

Mari Sandoz based her account of the Northern Cheyenne flight in *Cheyenne Autumn* (New York: Avon Books, 1953) on interviews with older tribal members, government documents, and George Bird Grinnell's description in *The Fighting Cheyennes* (Norman: University of Oklahoma Press, 1956), 398–428. See also John Stands in Timber and Margot Liberty, *Cheyenne Memories* (New Haven: Yale University Press, 1967), 231–37, and Donald J. Berthrong, *The Cheyenne and Arapaho Ordeal: Reservation and Agency Life in the Indian Territory, 1875–1907* (Norman: University of Oklahoma Press, 1976), 30–37.

Complete transcripts of Thomas Marquis's interviews are published in Thomas B. Marquis and Ronald Limbaugh, eds., *Cheyenne and Sioux: The*

Reminiscences of Four Indians and a White Soldier. Monograph 3 (Stockton, Calif.: Pacific Center for Western Historical Studies, 1973).

Helen Stauffer describes Mari Sandoz's discovery of Lost Chokecherry Valley in *Mari Sandoz, Story Catcher of the Plains* (Lincoln: University of Nebraska Press, 1988), 176. The place Sandoz identified as the site of Little Wolf's winter camp appears on modern maps as "Chokecherry Lake." However, some accounts place Little Wolf's camp as far as fifty miles south, near the headwaters of the Dismal River. See Charles Barron McIntosh, *The Nebraska Sand Hills: The Human Landscape* (Lincoln: University of Nebraska Press, 1996), 110.

Night

The epigraph on page 124 is attributed to the Pawnee chief Petalesharo by Martha Royce Blaine, *Pawnee Passage: 1870–1875* (Norman: University of Oklahoma Press, 1990), 259.

Black Elk talks about vision quests in Wallace Black Elk and William S. Lyon, *Black Elk: The Sacred Ways of a Lakota* (New York: Harper San Francisco, 1990).

Paul A. Johnsgard summarizes the role of owls in Native American and other belief systems in *North American Owls* (Washington, D.C.: Smithsonian Institution Press, 1988), 85–92.

A number of studies have demonstrated that birds have a remarkable ability to discriminate among individuals of their own and other species. See Paul Ehrlich, David Dobkin, and Darryl Wheye, *The Birder's Handbook* (New York: Simon and Schuster Fireside Books, 1988), 193–94.

Howard Ensign Evans describes the natural history of fireflies in *Life on a Little-Known Planet* (New York: Lyons and Burford, 1993), 102–15.

The closing poem is from Smithsonian Institution, *Bureau of American Ethnology Bulletin* 90 (Washington, D.C.: U.S. Government Printing Office, 1929), 126.

Plums in the Water

The story in which the Hidatsa express their disdain for people who eat rose hips (page 135) is excerpted in Kelly Kindscher, *Edible Wild Plants of the Prairie* (Lawrence: University Press of Kansas, 1992), 201. Kindscher discusses uses of chokecherries by Plains Indians on 176–82. Black Elk details their use in first menstruation ceremonies in *The Sacred Pipe: Black Elk's Ac-*

count of the Seven Sacred Rites of the Oglala Sioux, recorded and edited by Joseph Epes Brown (Norman: University of Oklahoma Press, 1953), 122–24. See also Bradford Angier, *Field Guide to Edible Wild Plants* (Harrisburg, Pa.: Stackpole Books, 1974), and Elias Yanovsky, *Food Plants of the North American Indians*, Miscellaneous Publication 237 (Washington, D.C.: U.S. Department of Agriculture, 1936).

David Wishart discusses Plains Indians' exploitation of bison for trade purposes in *An Unspeakable Sadness: The Dispossession of the Nebraska Indians* (Lincoln: University of Nebraska Press, 1994), 47.

The story of how the Cheyenne came to prosper on the plains is recounted in Karl Schlesier, *The Wolves of Heaven: Cheyenne Shamanism, Ceremonies, and Prehistoric Origins* (Norman: University of Oklahoma Press, 1987), 77, and in Richard Erdoes and Alfonso Ortiz, *American Indian Myths and Legends* (New York: Pantheon Books, 1984), 33–37.

See Henry David Thoreau, *Walden, or Life in the Woods* (Garden City, N.Y.: Anchor Books/Doubleday, 1973).

The story about Wihio and the plums is adapted from George Bird Grinnell, *By Cheyenne Campfires* (Lincoln: University of Nebraska Press, 1971), 282–83.

Riffraff

Sweet Medicine was a Cheyenne culture hero said to be born of a virgin. He reputedly performed miracles, taught the tribe righteous ways, and predicted the future. His words (quoted on page 147) are from John Stands in Timber and Margot Liberty, *Cheyenne Memories* (New Haven: Yale University Press, 1967), 27–41.

For details about red-headed woodpecker behavior, see Arthur Cleveland Bent, *Life Histories of North American Woodpeckers* (New York: Dover, 1964), 195–212. The effects of starlings on North American songbirds are discussed in Paul Ehrlich, David Dobkin, and Darryl Wheye, *The Birder's Handbook* (New York: Simon and Schuster Fireside Books, 1988), 489–93.

John Madson discusses the fate of North American tallgrass prairie in *Where the Sky Began* (Boston: Houghton Mifflin, 1982). For a thorough description of various types of prairie, see Ruth Carol Cushman and Stephen R. Jones, *The Shortgrass Prairie* (Boulder, Colo.: Pruett, 1988), 1–7.

Ponderosa forest expansion into Sandhills grasslands is described in

Ernest M. Steinauer and Thomas B. Bragg, "Ponderosa Pine Invasion of Nebraska Sandhills Prairie," *American Midlands Naturalist* 118 (1987): 358–65.

Blue Water

"How the Sioux Came to Be" is recounted by John Lame Deer in Richard Erdoes and Alfonso Ortiz, *American Indian Myths and Legends* (New York: Pantheon Books, 1984), 93–95.

Rex A. Smith presents a comprehensive description of the Sioux wars and the causes of the Wounded Knee Massacre in *Moon of Popping Trees* (Lincoln: University of Nebraska Press, 1975). For a more militant Lakota perspective, see Mary Crow Dog and Richard Erdoes, *Lakota Woman* (New York: Harper Perennial, 1990).

Lakota social activist Mark Monroe describes contemporary problems between Nebraska European Americans and Native Americans in *An Indian in White America* (Philadelphia: Temple University Press, 1994); the quotation is from 109.

Dune Dancers

The epigraph on page 169 by Chris Clarke appears in "Extinction and Health," *Earth Island Journal*, summer 1999, 20–22.

See Arthur Cleveland Bent, *Life Histories of North American Gallinaceous Birds* (New York: Dover, 1963).

Luther Standing Bear describes the dancing antics of prairie-chickens and grouse in *My Indian Boyhood* (Lincoln: University of Nebraska Press, 1988), 67–69.

Detailed accounts of the life histories and conservation status of grouse, prairie-chickens, and upland shorebirds appear in American Ornithologists' Union, *The Birds of North America*, 380 vols. (1992–) (Philadelphia: American Ornithologists' Union).

The story of the near extirpation and recovery of greater prairie-chickens in Illinois is detailed in Ronald L. Westemeier, Jeffrey D. Brawn, Scott A. Simpson, Terry L. Esker, Roger W. Jansen, Jeffrey W. Walk, Eric L. Kershner, Juan L. Bouzat, and Ken N. Paige, "Tracking the Long-Term Decline and Recovery of an Isolated Population," *Science* 282 (November 27, 1998), 1695–98.

The Lakota legend about Rabbit and the grouse is adapted from Marie McLaughlin, *Myths and Legends of the Sioux* (Lincoln: University of Nebraska Press, 1990), 20–23.

Purdum

Purdum's history is recounted in Dorothea W. Rogers, ed., *Purdum, Nebraska, Centennial, 1884–1984* (Purdum, Nebr.: United Church of Christ, 1984). The epigraph on page 180 is from an August 1997 interview with the author.

For more family histories, see Marianne B. Beel, *A Sandhill Century: A History of Cherry County, Nebraska* (Valentine, Nebr.: Cherry County Centennial Committee, 1986), vol. 2.

East Meets West

The epigraph on page 191 is from James Howard, in collaboration with Peter LeClaire, *Ponca Tribe* (Lincoln: University of Nebraska Press, 1995), 18.

Catlin is quoted in Helen Jackson, *A Century of Dishonor: A Sketch of the United States Government's Dealings with Some of the Indian Tribes* (St. Clair Shores, Mich.: Scholarly Press, 1974), 187. See also George Catlin, *Letters and Notes on the North American Indians*, edited and with an introduction by Michael McDonald Mooney (New York: Clarkson Potter, 1975).

David Wishart details the tragic fate of the Ponca tribe in *An Unspeakable Sadness: The Dispossession of the Nebraska Indians* (Lincoln: University of Nebraska Press, 1994), 83–86, 132–40, 141–53, and 202–16. See also Thomas H. Tibbles, *Standing Bear and the Ponca Chiefs*, edited and with an introduction by Kay Graber (Lincoln: University of Nebraska Press, 1972); Joseph Cash, *Ponca People* (Phoenix: Indian Tribal Series, 1975); and James Howard, *Ponca Tribe*. Chief Standing Bear's description of the tribe's relocation is quoted from Helen Jackson, *A Century of Dishonor*, 203.

Elizabeth Grobsmith and Beth Ritter describe the Ponca restoration in "The Ponca Tribe of Nebraska: The Process of Restoration of a Federally Terminated Tribe," *Human Organization* 51, no. 1 (1992): 1–16.

Transitions

The epigraph on page 209 is from John Madson, *Where the Sky Began* (Boston: Houghton Mifflin, 1982), 294.

The Snake River Falls Café recently changed managers. The friendly couple who currently run the place are well versed in local history as well as in Plains Indian medicine and folklore. The tour guide dog Mannix has passed on.

The interview with Ted Turner appeared in Paul Hammel, "Even in

'God's Own Cattle Country,' Turner Blazes Own Trail," *Omaha World-Herald*, October 17, 1998.

Anne Matthews writes about local reaction to the proposed "buffalo commons" in *Where the Buffalo Roam* (New York: Grove Weidenfeld, 1992). Daniel Licht makes a fascinating and convincing case for creating large grassland reserves on the Great Plains in *Ecology and Economics of the Great Plains* (Lincoln: University of Nebraska Press, 1997). For a comprehensive discussion of the importance of bison in prairie ecosystems, see Alan K. Knapp, John M. Blair, John M. Briggs, Scott L. Collins, David C. Hartnett, Loretta C. Johnson, and E. Gene Towne, "The Keystone Role of Bison in North American Tallgrass Prairie," *Bioscience* 48 (January 1999): 39–55.

Crescent Lake

The epigraph on page 222 consists of words attributed by Black Elk to the Buffalo Calf Maiden (also known as Fallen Star or Wohpe), who is said to have brought the sacred pipe and the seven sacred rites to the Lakota people. The source is Black Elk, *The Sacred Pipe: Black Elk's Account of the Seven Sacred Rites of the Oglala Sioux*, recorded and edited by Joseph Epes Brown (Norman: University of Oklahoma Press, 1953), 5–6.

The story about Wihio and the nighthawk is adapted from George Bird Grinnell's rendition in *By Cheyenne Campfires* (Lincoln: University of Nebraska Press, 1971), 301–2.

ACKNOWLEDGMENTS

In May 1986 my brother, Peter, and I drove up to western Nebraska to visit an archaeological dig that our father had worked on during the 1930s. We spent a night in the Sandhills sleeping under the stars and came away changed by the experience. I am grateful for Peter's constant encouragement, and for his understanding of my urge to wander over the hills.

In 1989 I visited Caroline Sandoz Pifer on her spectacular ranch south of Gordon, Nebraska. Over the ensuing years she shared her knowledge of the history and ecology of the Sandhills, introduced me to local ranchers, and helped me track down obscure places and sources. I thoroughly enjoyed and profited from our bird-watching excursions and far-ranging conversations.

Many other Sandhills area residents invited me into their homes or led me over the hills: Jack Grey Coon Armer, Bonnie Armer, Bob Cox, Lois Gibson, Mr. and Mrs. Keith Keys, Roxy Keys, Beryl Kuhre, Bob and Elaine Moreland, Adah Neubauer, Delmar Nielsen, Dorothea Rogers, Henry and Joan Rudnick, and Phil Wendzillo. Sandhills native Eleanor McClung shared a wealth of family reminiscences and settlers' stories.

Richard Nelson and Scott Taylor of the Nebraska Game and Parks Commission provided information about wildlife populations. Jim Swinehart and Mark Schroeder of the University of Nebraska Institute of Agriculture and Natural Resources took me out into the fens and patiently explained geological processes. Bill Behrends and his staff at Crescent Lake National Wildlife Refuge answered innumerable questions. Ken Strom of the National Audubon Society shared his love of cranes and his expertise in grassland ecology. Nature Conservancy ecologist Al Steuder imparted his intimate knowledge of the Niobrara River Valley. Carron Meaney and Anne Ruggles enlightened me on the origins of bison and domestic cattle.

I thank the many friends who accompanied me on trips, tracked down stray bits of information, or helped to clarify thoughts and theories: Audrey and Jim Benedict, Curt, Gaylon, and Karen Brown, Rachelle Canter, Ruth Carol Cushman, Mike Figgs, Randy Gietzen, Roger Jakoubek, Brian Jones, Kristala Kalil, Hugh Kingery, Jim Knopf, Jim McKee, Naseem Munshi, Dan Murphy, Pam Piombino, Michael Tupper, John Weller, Bob and Ru

Wing, and Tom Wolf. I am especially grateful for Christina Nealson's wisdom and encouragement and for Cynthia Kale's inspiration and support.

I value the critical comments of those who read drafts of the manuscript, including Marykay Cicio, Ruth Carol Cushman, Nancy Dawson, Merrill Gilfillan, Chris Hoffman, Cassandra Leoncini, Christina Nealson, and Ann Zwinger. I owe you.

Marty Dick, Arian Hampel, Cheryl Morris, and Trevor Munoz provided invaluable help in searching for pertinent books and articles, sorting slides, compiling data, and typing initial chapter drafts.

The enthusiasm and professionalism of Tom McCarthy, Alice Bennett, and D. A. Oliver, my editors at Ragged Mountain Press, made the publishing process smooth and enjoyable.

Finally, I could not have completed this manuscript without the loving help of my best editor, best friend, and "systems administrator" extraordinaire, my wife, Nancy Dawson. *Gracias por todo*, and much more.

GRATEFUL ACKNOWLEDGMENT is given the publishers and individuals for their permission to reprint the chapter epigraphs (full citations in the bibliographical essay).

Thanks also to Caroline Sandoz Pifer for permission to quote extensively from Caroline Sandoz Pifer, *Making of an Author: Mari Sandoz 1929–1930.* (Crawford, Nebr.: Cottonwood Press, 1982).